D0440041

"Is it really possible for one person to change the world? We all hear about the prominent billionaires who started huge businesses, but there are a few remarkable people with no desire for personal wealth, who saw a simple need and managed to find a way to transform the lives of millions. Don Schoendorfer and his wife encountered one woman crawling on her stomach in the streets of Morocco and never forgot her. That chance meeting spawned a simple idea: what if inexpensive wheelchairs could be designed and given to the millions of people who lack mobility, suffering in obscurity around the world? My prayer is that this story of the triumph of the human spirit will inspire others to imagine how they, too, might contribute to building a better world for those in need."

—RICHARD STEARNS, president emeritus of World Vision US, author of *The Hole in Our Gospel* and *Lead Like it Matters to God*

"When I stepped into the role of Senior Pastor at Mariners Church in 2018, I quickly heard about Don Schoendorfer and the amazing story of Free Wheelchair Mission. He has taken his gifts, talents, experience, and education and used them to serve others in simple yet profound ways. Don devotes himself to serving those around the world, many of whom would have never been able to venture out of a dark room. I'm incredibly thankful for his ministry, his labor, and the grit and tenacity he has shown in leading a nonprofit to tangibly serve the marginalized of this world. You will be inspired as you turn the pages of the riveting story of Don's life and the mission of Free Wheelchair Mission."

—ERIC GEIGER, senior pastor, Mariners Church

"Dr. Schoendorfer's story tells how providence led one man from humble beginnings through an MIT education and biomedical engineering research to a deep Christian faith and a mission that is transforming the lives of the poorest worldwide. I am proud of the modest part that MIT played in this moving story of how God can transform the talents of a Christian and his friends into a mission with global impact to help the poor. I read this book at a single sitting, which is something I never do, but the story was so compelling, I could not put it down."

—IAN HUTCHINSON, PhD, MIT professor of nuclear science and engineering, and author of *Can a Scientist Believe in Miracles?*

"Don's story struck a very personal nerve for my husband and me. We have a son who uses a wheelchair and we are well aware of the challenged life of someone living with disabilities. I was educated at Purdue University in special education long before our son's birth, and I desired to help those in need. Don's heart for the Lord and his mission to help others was a perfect fit for the foundation that we started for such purposes. We also have a global business with thousands of people who are eager to help financially and assist with wheelchair distributions internationally. The Lord put Free Wheelchair Mission and my husband and I together, and the result has been thousands of wheelchairs provided to those in need over the last fifteen years. Don's story goes way beyond the wheelchairs to include his life experiences and how God worked to make it all happen. It will change your life and perhaps give you food for thought as to what you might be able to do to change a life. When I started reading it, I could not put it down! It's a must-read!"

—NANCY DORNAN BERNFIELD, co-founder,
Network of Caring

"I love this book! Written in a way that captivates you from the beginning, this is a story of a curious young man who saw a need while traveling in Morocco. He used his gift of tinkering to do something. One man, with a vision given by God, made something unique for the world to be blessed by God. I pray that through this story, you too will be inspired and follow your own dream."

—ROBERT BARRIGER, lead pastor, Camino de Vida Church, Lima, Perú

"I am also lucky to have inhabited a similar world to Don's mission of providing wheeled mobility to those with limited means to purchase a wheelchair. When I first met Don years ago, I was struck by his humility, passion, and determination. His willingness to take on new ideas to improve the world for others has brought us closer together as colleagues and collaborators. I have worked in this same field for thirty years and count Don as one of my closest friends throughout this amazing journey we have both been on. I thoroughly recommend you read this book."

—DAVID CONSTANTINE, MBE, founder and director, Motivation Charitable Trust, UK

"Don's story is an inspiring example of how each of us has the power to improve the world around us. He has been a person capable of having a vision, carrying it out with tenacity and humility, and caring for those whom no one else cares about. Without a doubt, the world is a better place because of his journey. Don is an inspirational leader and it has been a blessing to be a part of this mission to give movement and hope to those who need it most. This book is an emotional and inspirational experience that teaches you that you don't have to help one million people to change the whole world. Start by changing one person's whole world."

—RICARDO FONT, former vice president of marketing and product management, Invacare Europe

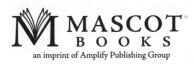

MASCOT
B O O K S
an imprint of Amplify Publishing Group

www.amplifypublishinggroup.com

Miracle Wheels: The Story of a Mission to Bring Mobility to the World

All net proceeds from the sales of this book go to support the ongoing work of Free Wheelchair Mission.

Some names, situations, and identifying details have been changed to protect the privacy of the people involved.

The views and opinions expressed in this book are solely those of the author. These views and opinions do not necessarily represent those of the publisher or staff.

For more information, please contact:
Mascot Books, an imprint of Amplify Publishing Group
620 Herndon Parkway, Suite 320
Herndon, VA 20170
info@amplifypublishing.com

Library of Congress Control Number: 2022909262

CPSIA Code: PRV0722A
ISBN-13: 978-1-63755-457-9

Printed in the United States

To the 75 million people in this world who are waiting for wheelchairs, and to all who, through their time, talent, and treasure, help to fulfill hopes and answer prayers.

MIRACLE WHEELS

The Story of a Mission to Bring Mobility to the World

DON SCHOENDORFER, PHD

WITH R. C. GEORGE

CONTENTS

FOREWORD

I grew up in Texas, and whenever I'd see Orange County, California, portrayed in movies and on television, I'd see images of carefree, beautiful people spending their days on the beach. They were living out the Southern California dream of luxury, expensive cars, and big mansions in the sun. At least, that's what I remember.

But as my wife, Tori, and I have spent more time in Orange County, having come to call the area our home in the off-season, we have seen a much different side. While some of what we see in the media is true, we now have many friends who are some of the most kind, caring, and selfless people we know.

Some of them are guys at my church. While having a conversation with them, I found that they seemed to really be on fire about a nonprofit mission based nearby, in Irvine, California. They talked about how there were millions of people around the world living with disabilities, who had to crawl or be carried everywhere they went. This organization, they said, manufactured wheelchairs and provided them at no cost to these individuals, giving them mobility and transforming their lives.

Their passion for this cause was contagious. I wanted to learn more.

Prior to learning about this problem, I had no idea that so many people were living without mobility. While visiting the Free Wheelchair Mission website, I watched heartbreaking videos and read moving stories about people with disabilities who were isolated in their homes or who had to crawl, sometimes through dust and dirt, just to get around in their day-to-day lives.

The more research I did, the more I saw that the wheelchairs provided by this mission were truly changing people's lives. Their new wheels were helping them break free from the isolation they were experiencing. With wheelchairs, they could see family again, go to school again. They could now go to work, go to church, and do so much more.

I also was intrigued by the story of Free Wheelchair Mission's founder, Dr. Don Schoendorfer, and how he had used his talents and his education to invent the ingenious wheelchairs that have now been provided to more than one million people around the world.

In learning all of this, I thought, "This is incredible. How have I not heard about this problem and Don's amazing wheelchairs sooner?"

I was so moved by Don's story and the work of Free Wheelchair Mission that I had to share it with Tori.

Tori lives with a condition called postural orthostatic tachycardia syndrome, or "POTS." This condition affects her blood circulation and can cause her to become severely lightheaded, dizzy, or nauseous, especially when she stands up. It mostly affects women, and, as Tori has met other women living with this condition, she knows firsthand how important wheelchairs are for many who are living with POTS.

When Tori learned that millions around the world, including women and children, have no access to wheelchairs, she was personally very moved by this cause. She couldn't even imagine what it would be like to not have access to a wheelchair for someone living with a disability.

When it comes to various charities and ministries, Tori and I are a team, and we both need to be united in our passions for the ones that we support. It took no time at all for us to want to step up to do what we could to get behind Don Schoendorfer and the work of Free Wheelchair Mission. Through our Foles Believe Foundation, we have been honored and proud to support this mission financially and through their Miracle of Mobility event.

The more I have come to learn about Don's story and the founding of Free Wheelchair Mission, the more Tori and I are touched and impressed by it. With many parallels to my own life and story, I've already learned a lot from Don and his heart to help those in need.

From his early days growing up in a small town in Ohio to what he's accomplishing today through his mission, Don's story is a powerful example of what can happen when we use our gifts to follow our unique purpose and calling.

God seemed to be preparing Don by giving him the talents, skills, and knowledge he would need later in life. It is also clear that God had placed many people in Don's life in the right places and at the right times: his parents, who impressed upon him the importance of education and instilled a sense of curiosity; his professors, who encouraged him despite many setbacks; his church community, which helped with starting his nonprofit; and his family and friends, who made such an impact at so many critical junctures in his life.

The world constantly tries to tell us what "success" looks like. So we might have big dreams and go down a road thinking that we need to make a lot of money or achieve certain standards set by the world. Then, God says, "I've given you all these gifts and experiences and placed all these people in your path for a reason. *This* is what you should be doing with what I've given you."

Don's character and values have made a significant impression on me. At an early age, he set big goals for himself and was motivated and driven to accomplish them. While he was gifted in so many ways, he still had to work hard: just like in football, you may have some raw abilities, but it takes a ton of hard work and years of training and experience to get to the top of your game.

Even for his many amazing accomplishments, Don is such a humble man, grounded by his faith. Like any great quarterback or leader, he knows his strengths, but he also recognizes he needs help from others. From the early days of Free Wheelchair Mission through today, Don has attracted a great team of talented people who have contributed greatly to their ongoing mission.

Don also forged ahead in his mission, despite many setbacks that may have ended the journey for others. I could see parallels in my own life, where I've faced trials with feelings of isolation, family illnesses, or unexpected changes that have tempted me to want to throw in the towel. For me, and for Don as well, it seems, those have been the times that we dropped to our knees in prayer for help, confessing that we cannot do it on our own. However, in Don's life and in mine, God continues to bring us through those dark days.

I'm grateful that Don forged through those challenges because his mission is so important. I have been especially inspired by so many of the stories of people's lives being transformed when receiving a wheelchair—stories like that of Julia in Armenia, who changed before Don's eyes from a sullen, shy little girl to a laughing, joyful child after being lifted into her very first wheelchair.

Don and his team at Free Wheelchair Mission have provided more than one million wheelchairs to those living with disabilities in developing countries. Think about how many millions of lives have been transformed through this, especially when you

Don Schoendorfer

consider the transformation that also takes place among families and in communities.

However, the needs are still great, unfortunately. An estimated seventy-five million people still need wheelchairs worldwide.

I've also learned that things like natural disasters, wars, and worldwide pandemics only make the situation more urgent. We may not realize this here in the US, but people living with disabilities in developing countries are often at higher risk in emergencies, so it is critical that they get access to wheelchairs in order to get medical attention or flee from danger.

Tori and I pray that you would be blessed and inspired by Don's book and the story of Free Wheelchair Mission. Just as Don demonstrated in his journey, you don't have to be rich and successful in the eyes of the world to have a tremendous impact on millions of people.

We hope you will do something with your own gifts and talents to help lift people with disabilities into brand-new wheelchairs, even if it's just sharing this book with others, volunteering, or participating in one of Free Wheelchair Mission's many events. If you can give at least one wheelchair to someone with a disability, please do. If you can give one or more wheelchairs every month, even better.

May this book be only the start of your new journey alongside Don and Free Wheelchair Mission. Together, we can transform lives with Don's miracle wheels and the gift of mobility.

Nick Foles
Super Bowl LII MVP
Fall 2021

"The most important thing anybody can do for us is to tell our story."

—Don Schoendorfer

PROLOGUE

Tétouan, Morocco
Summer 1979

I t only took a few seconds for a complete stranger—a woman I would never see again—to change my life forever.

It was the summer of 1979, and I was twenty-nine years old. Laurie and I were living outside Boston, with no kids and two stable jobs. Our friends had cautioned us against traveling to Morocco alone, but we were enjoying a two-week vacation in Spain, and adventure was calling. We rented a tan sedan in Gibraltar, crossed by ferry to Tangier, and embarked on the 220-mile drive down the cinematic coast to Casablanca, a popular travel destination for the young and hip.

Shortly before noon, we arrived at Tétouan, a medieval city nestled on the northern tip of Africa's coast. Nicknamed the "White Dove" for the color of its buildings, the city sloped out of the sea, rising first in a layer of brown and then in a layer of white before reaching up with its hills to touch the blue sky.

We parked our car outside the medina, the ancient Arab quarter of the city, hoping to see the sites and do some early Christmas shopping. We were looking, in particular, for the *babouche*—the quintessential Moroccan slip-on shoe famous for its plush, padded soles and comfortable leather interior. They'd make great gifts for our family back home. Everyone here had them on their feet, which gave us hope of finding them in the marketplace, one of the oldest in Morocco.

Tétouan was a city of locals, not tourists. The women were dressed in billowing layers of fabric, their eyes peering at us through narrow slits. The men wore skull caps and long wool robes that dropped to their ankles, not baggy but definitely loose. All the clothing was neutral, like the colors of the ground: tans, browns, grays, and blacks.

A gate marked the entrance to the fifteenth-century marketplace. It rose some thirty feet above us and passed directly through a fortress-thick medieval wall. I looked up at the openings that stippled the top of the wall, each about the span of a man's shoulders.

It was a pretty busy place, the marketplace—a good mixture of all ages, with little kids and older people all coming and going through the onion-shaped archway. The sides of the archway bulged widely before coming to a sudden point at the top, a slight difference from the Gothic arch I was familiar with.

This was our first exposure to Islamic architecture. The whole experience felt like we were stepping back in time, back to an era when thick walls wrapped all the way around the city, protecting its population from the arrows and catapults of Crusaders.

Somewhat unsure of our surroundings, Laurie kept one hand clutched to her brown leather satchel as we entered the narrow marketplace street. From side to side, it stretched about ten feet across, too small for a modern car. The street looked like it had a thousand years of wear on it. The cobblestones were uneven, worn smooth by centuries of shoes and the weight of wagon wheels. You had to watch your step. And I noticed the center of the street dipped low, forming a drain to accommodate the huge torrents of water that fell in the rainy season.

The road veined away from the parking lot, and we followed it deeper into the bazaar, where merchants lined the sides of the street, hawking wares from their stalls. It was a beautiful day, made all the more pleasant by the gentle breeze coming off the sea. The sky was a wide-open blue, broken only occasionally by intricate lattice roofs that carved the sun into tiny geometric shapes on the street.

I looked up at the two-story buildings that flanked our path. At first, I thought their walls were made of adobe, like something you'd see in Mexico. But when I looked closer, I realized that these walls belonged to an older age, when empires were built to last—when masons placed their stones with a sense of permanency, stones that could resist not only the attack of armies, but also the slow erosion of time. The rainy season couldn't melt these white-spackled walls. They looked like bones that history had recycled rather than buried.

I ran my eyes along the electrical wires that branched up the walls and over the doorways to connect hanging light bulbs to small holes in the wall where the lines disappeared. Near the tops of the walls were windows, most of them draped with drying laundry.

Modernity had barely touched this ancient alley.

We saw men charming cobras in the street. In the merchant stalls, sheep heads hung from hooks, along with plucked and unplucked chickens. Flies buzzed everywhere. The scent of fresh meat and leather hung in the air. We saw barrel-sized vats of dye, filled with colorful fabric.

Laurie and I shuffled from stall to stall, a blur of booths, and after a while, we began to lose our sense of direction. There were no right angles, really. The spine of the street was crooked. It followed an organic route over the terrain, with people spilling in from small alleys and doorways that wormed through the buildings.

A man walked by leading a donkey and cart, the cart's wheels bumping loudly over the corrugated cobblestones. My eyes went to the wooden axle, which creaked beneath the weight of its load. A primitive but effective design. *Stuck on with a wedge,* I observed.

We passed by another merchant selling pots and pans and all sorts of round, shiny objects. I caught our reflection in one of the plates.

Laurie was wearing a long-sleeved pullover and jeans. The Moroccan sun drew out red highlights in her strawberry-blonde hair, which she had tied up in a ponytail. Mine was shaggy. I had the beginnings of a beard on my chin, and I wore sunglasses and a short-sleeved collared polo tucked neatly into my Levis. Since we were traveling through unfamiliar territory, we had dressed down, not wanting to stick out.

But our modest efforts at keeping a low profile did nothing to prevent the locals from spotting us. We looked, to be sure, like tourists, and they had become very aware of our presence. They'd obviously seen the Portuguese license plate on our rental car and took us to be European travelers with money to spend. First, we'd hear someone yell, "Português!" and a few seconds later, we'd be surrounded by people wanting to give us tours and sell us things.

An unsettled feeling spread through my stomach as people swarmed us more aggressively, trying to take us with them. In the back of my mind, I began to question whether we had made the right decision to come to Tétouan. Maybe we should turn back. We had made no plans for the evening. Would we stay the night? If so, where? It wasn't like there was a Motel 6 around the corner. In fact, we didn't see anything that even remotely resembled a hotel. The longer we stayed, the more anxious we grew.

Don Schoendorfer

Then, the pungent smell of meat gave way to the sweet aroma of spices.

Gusts of cinnamon and cardamom wafted up the street, carried by the breeze, snapping us back to our feeling of adventure. We lingered around the booths, inhaling the fragrant spices, which the merchants displayed in large burlap sacks. Each row of sacks was elevated at a different height to showcase the vibrant bursts of reds, greens, yellows, and purples—a cornucopia of powdered color set against the backdrop of the neutral walls and dusty street.

It was also melon season in Morocco, we discovered. We followed our noses to another booth brimming with fresh cantaloupe. The merchant saw us coming, too, and with one lightning-fast slice of his blade, he chopped open the melon for us to sample.

We still felt unsettled. But with each bite of cantaloupe, and with each new booth, sight, and smell, Laurie and I welcomed the new, unfamiliar experience. The whole afternoon, like that delicious melon, was ripe with possibility. And hopefully, somewhere in the maze of this ancient medina, we'd find our holy grail—those elusive leather slippers.

That's when I saw her.

She was about twenty feet from us, lying flat on her stomach, belly on the ground, pulling herself across the uneven cobblestones. Her hands were dirty and bloodied, covered with cuts and open blisters. I looked at her feet, which were limp and torn. Her legs dragged behind her body as she clawed her way, inch by inch, to the edge of the street.

It took me a few seconds to fully grasp this woman's misery.

She weighed no more than a hundred pounds, I'd guess. Probably in her thirties, maybe younger. I couldn't tell because she kept her face low, staring forward at the ground. But she seemed to know where she was going, and I got the impression that she was trying to cross the street, waiting for an opening to emerge in the bustling crowd.

From her vantage point, only a few inches off the ground, it must have looked like a sea of feet rushing by, a current of shoes and legs and fast-moving hazards to avoid. People were spilling around her as she kept her limbs close, trying to avoid being trampled.

This wasn't the first time that I'd seen something like this. While traveling through Europe, I'd seen amputees and others who couldn't walk sliding across the ground on skateboards and makeshift devices that offered some measure of mobility.

But the sight of this woman stopped me cold in my tracks. She wasn't just sliding *across* the ground. She was sliding *on* the ground itself. This woman, propelled only by her upper body, couldn't even get up on her knees to crawl.

There was nothing between her and the ground, nothing to separate her tiny torso from the dirt and grime. Her tattered clothes had absorbed all the tans, browns, and grays of the dusty street, making her blend in, virtually indistinguishable from the cobblestones. She was almost invisible.

The crowd was sweeping us down the street, unfazed by the woman's plight, so we stepped back against a nearby wall. *Is anybody going to do anything about this?* I wondered. *Is everybody just going to ignore her?*

"We have to do something," I said to Laurie, trying to keep my voice low so as not to draw the attention of the people hurrying by. She nodded, obviously thinking the same thing. We looked up and down the street, craning our necks to scan the shops nearby, searching for something to buy her, anything with wheels.

We have to get her off the ground, I kept thinking.

People kept rushing past her, avoiding her as if she were somehow defiled. But before we could gather our thoughts and figure out a way to help her, she was gone. The woman had vanished into the crowd. I took Laurie's hand as we stepped back into the street, stunned into silence by what we'd just seen.

As the day turned to dusk, Laurie and I abandoned our quest of finding those leather shoes, which now seemed so trivial. We turned our thoughts instead to finding shelter for the night.

The sun dipped below the hills of Tétouan, emptying the sky of its blue until darkness spread its wings over the city of the White Dove.

The memory of that woman lingered in my mind. The way she dragged her body. The open sores on her legs. The scabs. The blood. The blisters on her hands. The way the crowd ignored her. As I drifted to sleep that night, the image of her small, broken torso—invisible to the people around her—haunted my thoughts. The shock of watching her make her way through the street distressed me almost as much as our inability to do anything about her situation. *If only we could have found a way to help her,* I thought, my eyelids growing heavy. Finally, I closed my eyes, knowing we would never see her again. Our chance to help had passed.

Decades later, long after we had left Morocco and returned to our jobs, long after we had grown our family and built our careers, her memory would surface once again. The seed planted in Tétouan would eventually blossom into a blueprint.

1

SPEED

Ashtabula, Ohio
August 1959

I felt the adrenaline surge through my ten-year-old body as I picked up speed in my go-kart: ten, fifteen, twenty miles an hour.

It wasn't a fancy go-kart, like the kind you'd see at the county fair or in the catalogues. *Wow*! I'd think, cutting out pictures of those shiny, modern machines, professionally made and properly balanced. *Wouldn't it be great to have one of those*! But to a kid like me, growing up in a blue-collar neighborhood, in a blue-collar city, those hundred-dollar go-karts might as well have been sports cars. I definitely couldn't afford one of those. But a few years earlier, I'd managed to save up seven dollars from my paper route to buy my go-kart.

It was more of a tricycle, actually: two smaller wheels with a fan belt running to a pulley on the left wheel. The engine, a Briggs & Stratton lawn mower motor, was bolted to a large piece of plywood. On the front of the plywood, I'd mounted a bicycle frame, minus the rear wheel and pedals. I sat on the bicycle seat and steered with the handlebars that were connected to the bicycle wheel, the third wheel of my tricycle.

I wasn't ashamed of the way the go-kart looked. It was utilitarian and really ugly—kind of a piece of junk—but it gave me speed and mobility, and that's all that really mattered.

The houses on West Eighth Street began to blur as I whipped the handlebars sharply to the right, turning out of my neighborhood and onto Ohio Avenue. As usual, I took the corner as fast as I could, fast enough for the go-kart to lean heavily to the left, its back wheel lifting up and then coming down again. Directly in front of me was Lake Erie, its wide shoreline only two blocks from my house.

When I approached the lake, I peeled onto Walnut Boulevard, the wind in my face, flapping through the holes in my tattered shirt. I gave it the gun, forcing the trike to reach its maximum speed—a whopping twenty-five miles per hour.

It was an easy place to live, Ashtabula. You wouldn't really call it urban, not in the 1960s. But it wasn't exactly rural either. It was an idyllic place where you could get away with all sorts of mischief. No one seemed to care, for example, that a ten-year-old kid was tearing through town on a super-loud, souped-up tricycle. No one except the police.

My three-wheeled go-kart was traveling on land that once belonged to William Hubbard, a well-known abolitionist who moved from New York to Ashtabula in 1840. He purchased fifty-eight thousand acres near Lake Erie and used his home to shelter runaway slaves.

I glanced to my left as I passed Hubbard's two-story house. He provided asylum for fugitives here, hiding them in his basement. When it was safe, he escorted them a quarter mile to his warehouse, where ferry boat captains waited eagerly to take them to Canada, to freedom on the other side of the wide blue lake.

I drove across the Ashtabula River, not far from where the "Ashtabula Train Disaster" had occurred nearly a century earlier. In 1876, a train carrying one hundred and sixty passengers was crossing

Don Schoendorfer

the river when the bridge, having been poorly engineered, suddenly collapsed. The train plunged into the river, its coal-fired stoves and oil lamps setting the wooden carriages on fire. Ninety-two people perished. The disaster put our little town on the national map—the worst rail accident in the history of the United States. Everyone knew about the "Ashtabula Horror," as it was called, especially my father, a railroad man himself.

Born in Coudersport, Pennsylvania, in the year 1900, my father spent his childhood in the country, growing up in the mountainous middle of Pennsylvania, not far from a train depot for the New York Central Railroad. When he was in the eighth grade, his parents figured he'd had enough education, so he began a three-year apprenticeship with the railroad, starting off at thirteen cents an hour.

The job kept him occupied, gave him some spending money, and allowed him to help support his family. When he finished his training, he began working as a machinist, raising his hourly wage to eighteen cents. It was steady work, working on train engines. He was in charge of blueprinting, designing, and manufacturing intricate machinery. Because of his friendly disposition and generous spirit—he was a man quick to smile and always willing to lend a hand—somewhere along his forty-nine-year career with the New York Central he eventually worked his way up to foreman.

Tragedy marked my father's early adulthood. By the time he met my mother, a legal secretary who was seven years younger, he'd been married and widowed twice. His first wife died during childbirth, along with their baby, and his second was a physician who soon succumbed to cancer.

Unsurprisingly, my father developed a bit of a drinking problem. It didn't happen often, and my father never became violent or abusive, but about twice a year he'd come home pretty toasted.

"You know," my uncle Frank once told me, "your father's had a pretty rough life. I'm sure he's never told you about it, but there are a lot of things . . ." His voice trailed off, and a moment passed. "Every now and then, he just needs to have too much to drink."

One night when I was about twelve, he came home drunk. I heard a loud ruckus and grabbed my pellet gun. I wasn't really worried about my father. It was the guy bringing him home from the bar who concerned me. To me, it was terrifying. But to my mother, it was a huge embarrassment.

We had a happy family, even though my parents were occasionally at odds with each other. They slept in separate bedrooms, though that was common back in the day, and they tried to conceal their emotions in front of the kids.

We were never a very tight, emotional, or intimate family. Only twice did I see my mother cry—once when Christmas carolers came to the house, and the other time when my middle brother announced he'd eloped. She rarely let her feelings get the best of her. But when my father came home drunk, she'd grow furious. I could hear them arguing. They'd get a divorce, she'd threaten, as soon as I graduated from high school.

My father was five foot nine, thin, and had "tennis-ball-gray" hair. He wore plain clothes most days, only getting dressed up to go to church at the Second Congregational Church in Ashtabula. My mother had become the church secretary, and my father put his skills to good use as a sexton tasked with maintaining the church building. My brothers and I attended Sunday School and the church service, and on most Sundays, my parents had to struggle against all sorts of shenanigans as we tried to get out of going. I struggled to see how God was especially relevant to my life, but my father faithfully brought us to church every Sunday.

Don Schoendorfer

My father smiled a lot. He was high energy and loved music, and he taught my brothers to play the violin and the baritone trumpet. He played the bass fiddle in the orchestra and even marched, along with his own father, in parades, as a member of John Philip Sousa's famed band.

I remember one day when he came home, he couldn't talk because he'd had all of his teeth pulled out. Back then, people would get to a point where they couldn't afford to keep their teeth. I don't think people usually had them *all* pulled out, but my father did. He decided it was easier to just get it handled all at once. After he got dentures, he always looked a little bit different to me.

My mother was the dominant figure in the marriage. When she was in her twenties, she worked as a legal secretary in New York City and was very successful and adventuresome. Before she married, she had a vacation home on Long Island and a shiny convertible. In 1932, long before interstates crisscrossed the country, she took her mother on vacation out west, driving that convertible on dirt roads all the way to California.

My parents met on a dude ranch, married in 1939, and went camping for their honeymoon. They had lived through the Great Depression and, like everyone else, had lost what little money they'd had when the stock market crashed. "Donnie," my mother would say, "you have to invest in education. That's the one thing they can't take away from you. Diamonds, gold—they'll take it all, but not your education."

They were survivors, both of them, and they taught me to buy things only when you had the money. Debt wasn't an option. Under no circumstance should you borrow anything from anyone. Ever.

They settled in Albany, where I was born in 1949, five years after the arrival of my middle brother and nearly a decade after my oldest brother was born. A few years later, my father ended up losing his job but got a new one in Ohio, some five hundred miles west. Back then, the railroad would give employees a pass to take the train for free, sometimes even in a Pullman car, so every week he'd commute from Albany to Ohio, about twelve hours each way. Eventually, this routine grew tiresome, and my parents moved the family to Ashtabula.

There were no moving vans, but we didn't have much furniture. Everything we had went into an eight-foot trailer towed by our Pontiac, by then already two decades old. My mother drove all three of us in that car, and every time we stopped for dinner, my brothers would act up, and chaos would ensue. I'm sure I was no angel, either.

"I'm never taking you kids to a restaurant again!" she'd swear. And for twenty-three hours a day, she meant it.

We never had a lot of money and were constantly fixing things. When something stopped working, we'd just keep repairing it. The toaster, the clock, the washing machine . . . I felt sorry for the poor appliances in our house. We kept bringing them back to life. We'd never let them die.

Our cars were also doomed to this sort of purgatory. My father was good at fixing things. "There's always a way to make things work," he told me. When it came to mechanical and electrical repairs, there was never a shortage of wrenches, screwdrivers, and tools at our disposal.

My mother didn't like it very much, all of the tinkering and repairs. But she put up with it because that was the only option we had.

———————————

The lake on my left, the wind in my face, I continued whipping my go-kart across town, feeling invincible, unstoppable.

But then, I spotted it: a police car, coming toward me from the

Don Schoendorfer

opposite direction, growing larger with each second. The officer passed me, a puzzled expression on his face.

A few harrowing seconds passed. I held my breath. Then, he switched on his siren.

My go-kart didn't have a rearview mirror, so I shot my head around to see the red lights flashing behind. He was right on my tail, coming up fast. I was in big trouble.

Here we go again.

This wasn't the first time the police had chased me, and it probably wouldn't be the last. It was a calculated risk, but I'd outrun the cops before. With any luck, I could do it again. My neighborhood wasn't far away. All I needed was a side street, some alley or driveway to disappear into, and then, once the patrol car passed, I'd be able to zip home, swerve my go-kart into the garage, roll the door shut, and hide.

The lawn mower engine screamed as I squeezed every bit of energy from the one-and-a-half horsepower motor. I jerked the handlebars, turned into a neighborhood, bounded down the street and through the stop sign, eased up to turn left onto another road, and gunned the gas like my life depended on it.

The sound of the siren grew weaker as I zigzagged home, craning my neck, taking all kinds of turns, thinking only of that one thing: the garage where I could ditch the kart.

My back wheel lifted off the street as I took the curve. Now I was back on West Eighth, and my head was dizzy from the adrenaline. A few neighbors watched me race by. They'd seen me do this before, and I could almost feel their eyes on me, wondering if this time would be different.

My house was fast approaching. Too fast. Once again, I'd mistimed my approach. This was going to be a big problem because my go-kart suffered from one significant deficiency.

It didn't have any brakes.

Going fast was never the issue. Stopping? Well, that was a different story.

I jerked the handlebars sharply to the right. The unstable trike flipped onto its side and began to roll, tumbling over itself. I tucked my head and held on tight, my arms scraping against the jagged asphalt, my jeans tearing and ripping even more.

The go-kart rolled twice, then a third time, until finally it came to a halt upside down on top of me. But there was no time to survey the damage. I had to kill the engine. I dragged myself out from under it, squirreled to the other side, cleaved the spark plug off, and then pulled out all the wires. The carburetor gummed up. The engine hummed, then sputtered, and finally died.

I hoisted the go-kart upright and muscled it up the driveway and into our garage. Across the street, two neighbors were shaking their heads at each other.

"This kid is never gonna learn."

2

BLUEPRINTS

Ashtabula, Ohio
March 1960

"Donnie, are you sure you want it to look that way?"

I glanced up at my father and nodded. My go-kart was in desperate need of an upgrade, and this was my third attempt at sketching the modifications. They finally looked perfect.

This wasn't the first time I'd tried my hand at drawing. Whenever I needed to explain something to my mother, she knew just how to help me communicate: "Draw me a picture, Donnie," she'd say. It was much easier to draw my dreams, or scenes from my imagination, or something I'd seen but didn't know what to call, than to try to explain them with words.

Occasionally, I'd receive chemistry sets as birthday or Christmas gifts, but it seemed that no matter the intended result, my experiments only produced puddles of black ink. The instructions included far too much reading, and I was a poor reader with mild dyslexia that haunted my efforts. Books never did anything for me, but using my hands—that's how I came alive.

I loved everything mechanical. If something was broken, I'd take it apart, investigate the gears and connections, and figure out how things worked. Broken radios, small appliances, hand tools, and clocks—as long as they were beyond repair, my parents gave me free rein, and I'd be occupied for hours.

My older brothers' Erector Sets were the ultimate, the most fascinating things in the world. I'd play with them endlessly, connecting metal beams to electric motors, bolting gears to thin sheets of metal. It was the perfect toy for a boy like me, who had the patience to construct but couldn't be bogged down by pages of exhaustive directions.

I was always missing pieces from the sets I'd inherited, sets that had been passed down twice by the time they reached me, but I filled my afternoons building and creating dynamic structures, animated by a little ingenuity.

One Christmas, my parents gave me the granddaddy of Erector Sets. The big steel box must have weighed forty pounds. It had treads and parachutes, and I built sturdy tanks and recreated the jump tower from the amusement park at the Chicago World's Fair.

What I liked about Erector Sets was that the box didn't give any details. The makers provided a picture, usually a pretty grubby photograph or simple sketch, and there was nothing I had to read.

Now, though, standing in front of my father, I found myself on the other end of the process. Instead of constructing from a picture, I'd become the one tasked with creating the drawing. And my go-kart depended on my ability to get it right.

When I was about seven years old, I'd realized that the reason my father could bring me to his railroad machinist shop was because he was the foreman. His shop was huge, thousands of square feet, with machinery and scrap metal everywhere.

One afternoon, when visiting the shop, I saw an enormous machine designed to chew up dilapidated railroad cars. To me, it looked like a hungry monster. My eyes darted over the monitors, gauges, and switches that controlled it. A man crawled on top to oversee the slow chomps of the hydraulic jaw as it bit off huge pieces of steel.

My father introduced me to the machinists who worked for him. I stuck out my little hand to shake their calloused, oil-stained palms. For weeks, these men had been helping me upgrade my go-kart. During his coffee breaks, my father would say, in passing, "Hey, Bill, would you mind making this for my son?" Nothing was too complicated for them. It only took the machinists about ten minutes to convert scrap metal into something I could use.

By the time I was twelve, I'd already modified the go-kart several times. Despite my many crashes, my parents never said that it was too dangerous. They always gave us a lot of freedom.

You could hear my go-kart coming from a mile away, just the way I wanted. I'd experimented with different types of mufflers, some quieter than others, but I wanted the sound to be louder, more obnoxious. For added stability, I knew that I needed to convert the tricycle into a four-wheeled vehicle.

In the evenings, after school and homework were complete, I worked on my designs. My plans called for parts that couldn't be purchased at a local hardware store. They had to be custom. My father knew that, and he also knew that a simple sketch wouldn't do. The blueprints had to be accurate.

My first drawing was full of mistakes. I crumpled the piece of paper into a ball and threw it away. The second one looked better to me, so I delivered it to my father, who studied it for a moment.

"Donnie, they can't make this," he said, pointing to the smudged piece of paper. "It's not possible." My brow furrowed, and I shot him a confused glance.

"Your drawing shows holes to drill," he continued, "but there's nothing to drill them into. You've drawn the holes, but not the actual part."

I took his advice and got back to work.

"This drawing isn't very neat," he said, looking at my revised sketches. "Why don't you try to clean it up a bit?"

Back to the drawing board. I made another copy and presented it to him.

"Donnie, are you sure you want it to look that way? They're going to machine exactly what you draw, and they don't know what you're trying to create."

In reality, my father knew that the machinists would have figured out that I was trying to make a go-kart. They had children of their own. But my father had a lesson for me, and he was going to make sure that I learned it.

"Okay," he said, "I'm going to tell them to make what you've drawn here. Are you sure this is right?"

I nodded more firmly than ever, confident this time.

The next evening, I heard the rumble of my father's car, a rusted-out 1949 Mercury, as it pulled into the driveway. He had come home from work. I ran to the front door, excited to see how my new part turned out. He pulled the customized hinge from his bag and handed it to me. I examined it, feeling the knot in my stomach, the nervousness, growing larger.

"Dad, they didn't make the part right! There's no way this will fit my go-kart."

My father removed my blueprints from his lunch box. "Why don't you look at the drawing and compare it to your part," he said. "Then, tell me what's wrong with it."

I surveyed the drawing, comparing it to the hinge. Instantly, I saw my mistakes. My heart sank. "I'm sorry, Dad. I got the guys to make the wrong thing."

"Do you want to try again?" he asked. "They won't give up if you won't." My father smiled at me, playfully tousling my hair. "Do the drawing, Donnie, and make it right."

———————

I never did add brakes to the go-kart. Didn't see the point. But there *was* one final thing I needed to install. I searched everywhere for the missing part—inside the rooms of my house, in the garage, behind the old furniture stashed in the attic.

Then I saw it: a white plastic chair. It was out in the backyard, exposed to the elements, neglected and grimy. I picked it up and appreciated how light it was. Then I wiped the dirt off the seat and examined the material. It looked durable, like it could take a beating. The chair needed to be capable of enduring abuse.

This'll do nicely, I thought. Plus, it was waterproof.

I picked up the chair, carried it to the garage, wiped off the remaining dirt, and then sat down, putting my whole weight against its frame, feeling the sturdy back support. I only needed the seat of the chair, so I got to work unscrewing the legs.

Gone were the days of sitting directly on the plywood. Now I could cruise the city in style, sitting in the lap of luxury. It was a dream come true.

Little did I know how significant a similar white plastic chair would one day be.

3

STYLE

Ashtabula, Ohio
September 1960

My mother wanted me to be like Uncle George when I grew up.

She viewed him as a prince of a man: a tall, clean-shaven Irishman, neat and tidy, sophisticated and soft-spoken, with bright-red hair and a rigid, formal posture. He was married to my mother's sister, and even back then, it bothered me that my uncle—not my father—was my role model, the standard I was expected to emulate.

"Don't do anything you'll be afraid to tell Uncle George," my mother would warn.

Uncle George had discriminating opinions about everything from food to the government, and he'd often share them while dipping his bagels into coffee at the many restaurants and diners he frequented.

Everyone knew him. He was a successful businessman in New York City, and though he could have afforded much more, he lived in a modest apartment in New Jersey and commuted to work at a firm in Manhattan.

He was something of a genius, too, able to devour a whole book in a single day. Sometimes I'd see him go into the bathroom with a book and not return for hours.

Uncle George had a vacation home on the Jersey coast where I'd spend my summers, and every time I saw him, he'd be perfectly attired: a pressed suit, crisp white shirt, polished shoes for work, and smart slacks with polos and cardigans on the weekends. Uncle George sure knew how to dress for the occasion. He was the hero I was expected to impress, and in the sixth grade, I finally got my chance.

Since Uncle George always dressed up for work, I decided to improve my own wardrobe. I committed to wearing a white dress shirt to school every morning. This irritated my mother since she had to iron them, but she indulged my newfound sense of style, grateful that I'd given up the tattered, bloodied clothes of my early go-kart days.

My mother believed it was important for her children to grow up with an appreciation of the arts. She insisted on decorating our home with crystal orbs and golden cups that she'd collected over the years, along with the huge paintings that her boss in New York City had once given to her. Things were displayed prominently and publicly, even if it meant putting them in places where they could be broken by her three rambunctious boys. For example, we had to be extremely careful when opening the blinds, lest the stained-glass art in the windows tip off the windowsill and shatter on the floor.

My mother's most prized possessions, by far, were the two chairs in the living room. She kept them wrapped in plastic coverings and treated them like they belonged in a museum. No one was ever allowed to sit in them because, as my mother was quick to explain to guests, these chairs had once adorned the château of Marie Antoinette.

For years, we all fell for it. We were totally convinced that *our* living room chairs had once supported the royal backsides of kings and queens. And even my mother believed it, or at least we thought she did. Maybe she hoped that by having things she considered valuable around, her children would gain a healthy appreciation of, if not an outright reverence for, the fine arts.

My parents were both charming, in their own ways. My father was dashing, and my mother was very attractive, even glamorous. In her thirties, people said she looked like a movie star. They didn't have much money, but my parents were always generous and willing to go the extra mile for someone in need.

Holidays were celebrated well, and Halloween was a time when my mother's creativity surged. She went to great lengths each year to design the most elaborate costumes for us to wear, and once I went trick-or-treating as a box of Lucky Strike cigarettes. From the waist down, you could see my legs. But from the waist up, I was a living, breathing cardboard box of smokes, standing four feet tall and wrapped in cellophane.

My mother went out of her way to prepare huge holiday dinners. Long before I could carry a gun, I'd join my father and brothers on their snowy Thanksgiving Day hunts, and by the time we got back, there would be plates full of warm appetizers waiting for us.

"Now, don't forget," she'd warn us, "we have dinner coming up, too!"

She took cooking seriously, and she knew how to prepare a traditional meal, but my mother also had an eclectic side to her personality, a spontaneous and rebellious streak. She could be a nonconformist when she wanted to. During Christmas, for example, she prepared a traditional goose or duck, served on her fine china, but she would also find a recipe she'd heard of from Denmark or Belgium and serve us something completely unexpected.

My father was much more conventional. *Do an honest day's work, and you'll have a good life.* But my mother would encourage us boys to think differently, challenging the arbitrary processes of our local school system and pushing people to consider alternatives. I marveled at her anecdotes, amazed by this woman who wouldn't take "because that's the way we've always done it" for an answer. I heard these stories from her, but I heard them from other people, too. "Donnie," they'd say, "sometimes your mother is just a little hard to deal with."

———

When I got to be old enough, my mother went back to work, and all the money she earned went back into the family. My father's wages paid the bills, but my mother's paid for some fun.

Each summer, after she'd saved up some money, my mother would pile the family in the car for vacation. My parents would drive us east to Buffalo and then a couple hundred miles north to a lake across the Canadian border, where we'd rent a cabin and a couple of fishing boats. My mother would bring a big cast-iron skillet and load it up with onions and potatoes with the hope that somebody would catch a fish before lunch.

When our finances became slim, my parents would gather us around the kitchen table for a family meeting. "Well, we're getting a little tight," they'd say, "and we just want to tell you that we're going to have to cut back on overspending for food. It's nothing to worry about, but we're not each going to have a pork chop."

This didn't bother me. I liked potatoes anyway.

———

Don Schoendorfer

One summer afternoon, as I was guiding our lawn mower across the front yard, my dad ambled over and stood quietly. I killed the engine, wiped the dripping sweat from my brow, and waited for him to speak.

"Donnie, I really hope you get to the point where you realize how important it is to have someone else mow your lawn for you."

Why would that matter? I wondered. "I don't see why that's important," I said, surprised. He smiled and walked away, leaving me to mull over his comment. From his perspective, it was important to reach the point in life where you can hire out household tasks. I chewed on his words, turning them over in my head as the blades of the mower sliced the grass. I later realized what he was trying to tell me.

Donnie, I hope you're aiming for a higher standard of life than I've achieved.

4

THE NEWSPAPER

Ashtabula, Ohio
December 1960

I squeezed between my two older brothers as we slid into the back of our rusted-out sedan, a car that really had no business being on the road.

My father didn't dabble too much in car mechanics, but he'd managed to keep the thing running for his commute back and forth to the machine shop. The vehicle was, quite literally, falling apart. We had to bolt one of the doors shut because we were afraid it was going to fall right off on the open road.

I peered down between my feet and through the gaping hole in the floorboard, watching the ground start to move as my dad revved the engine and rolled back out of the Ashtabula train station parking lot.

It was Sunday afternoon, after church, and we were pulling out of the same station where the ill-fated train had departed nearly a century earlier before crashing some one thousand feet down the line.

My father never exceeded an eighth-grade education. My mother, though she never had the privilege of formal education, loved learning on her own. As a carry-over from their time living in New York, every week my parents drove the family to the train station to buy a freshly printed copy of the *New York Times*. It was a big deal, the Sunday edition. The newspaper was a good two inches thick, must have weighed a couple of pounds, and if you wanted to read it from start to finish, it would take the better half of a day.

My parents adored that newspaper and the lively conversation its articles elicited. When we'd get home, they'd devour every single page and spend the rest of the afternoon discussing current events, scrutinizing the opinion pieces, and debating politics. I loved listening to their intellectual exchanges, the way they challenged each other's opinions and talked about developments in far corners of the world.

None of us boys were really that smart, as measured in the conventional way of public education, but my older brothers wanted to be engineers, having grown up fixing things around the house with our father. The trajectory of their education was set in stone. My older brother Carl spent four years studying at a liberal arts college some seventy miles to the west. It was a fine, small, Methodist liberal arts college, Baldwin Wallace, but it had an agreement with Columbia University through which he'd be able to study the necessary engineering coursework and end up with a master's degree in both liberal arts and engineering.

I wasn't really working hard. I hated studying and couldn't care less about the Bs and Cs my teachers gave me. The whole idea of school didn't interest me in the slightest. I wasn't a strong student, and instead of sitting inside a classroom listening to lectures all day, there were other things I'd much rather spend my time doing.

"You need to make a choice, Donnie," my mother said to me one day, sitting me down for a serious discussion. "If you want to go to college, you need to come up with better grades, and some money. By the time we get your two brothers through school, we won't have any left." I looked over at my father, who seemed to agree. "Academically, you're just not doing well," she continued. "You're just getting by."

But if I wanted to be like Uncle George, I knew that the most direct path to his New York City lifestyle was through Baldwin Wallace. To do that, I needed to turn a corner, hunker down, study harder, and get my grades in shape. I also probably needed to start saving money. My oldest brother was going off to college, so I decided to take over his paper route. If my parents were right about the money running out, and I suspected they were, I'd need to save up for tuition fees.

The alternative future looked bleak to me: living in Ashtabula for the rest of my life and becoming a factory worker or a longshoreman for the thriving iron ore and rubber shipping port of Lake Erie's Ashtabula harbor. They were noble ways to earn a living, but I wasn't interested in those options, in that lifestyle.

There I was, going into eighth grade, living in a backwater town on the edge of Lake Erie where everyone looked the same because we all bought our clothes from the one clothing store in Ashtabula. Unlike so many of my classmates, who would get married right out of high school, start a family, and never leave, I wanted to look different, to be different. Ashtabula was a perfect, idyllic place to grow up, but I had a burning desire to do something else with my life, even if I didn't know what that was going to be.

———————

We arrived home with a copy of the Sunday *New York Times*, and I began reading. Suddenly, my eyes landed on an intriguing article. The writer claimed that MIT—the Massachusetts Institute of Technology in Cambridge—was the best engineering school in the world. I felt the sudden rush of excitement as I repeated those words over and over in my head. *The best? In the entire world?*

I scoured every word of the article, taking it all in, looking at the photos of the school library and its enormous Great Dome soaring overhead, all the while feeling that I was holding my entire future in my hands. Everything I ever wanted—my purpose, my destiny, my dream—was right there between my fingers, incarnated in ink, a blueprint of things to come.

"Mom," I announced, pointing to the page, "when I go to college, I want to go *here!*"

She picked up the newspaper and examined it. "Then why don't you write them? See what you can find out?"

I dashed to my room, grabbed a pencil, and wrote a handwritten letter to MIT on my drafting table. I folded the paper, slipped it into an envelope, scribbled down the mailing address—"MIT, New England"—and then darted as fast as my legs could carry me to the mailbox.

After depositing my dream, I returned to my room and cut the advertisement out of the newspaper. I hung it prominently on the wall above my bed, the last thing I'd see before falling asleep at night.

Nothing was going to stop me from making this dream come true—not school, not grades, not money. Education was my way out, my great escape, my portal to a life of significance. And from that moment on, I didn't look back. I'd study twice as long, work twice as hard. I'd do anything and everything I could to get into MIT, which was, after all, according to the *New York Times*, the best engineering school in the world.

Once I arrived at high school, my academic vision required a new wardrobe, so I thought.

"I'm tired of looking like everybody else in this small town," I told my mother, knowing full well that she'd understand.

She was a brilliant seamstress, my mother, creative and industrious. I'd see her browse through the magazine section of the newspaper, clipping out inspirations and recreating them on her sewing machine. This habit of hers, of replicating clothes she saw, started when she lived in New York.

She didn't have a lot of money, so she'd go window shopping along Fifth Avenue and draw sketches of the fancy dresses she saw in the storefronts. Then she'd go to the fabric district, purchase the fabric she'd seen, and the next morning, after spending the night sewing, she'd show up wearing the very latest from the windows of Bergdorf Goodman and Saks.

My mother recognized this same quirkiness in me. She embraced my desire to look different from the locals, and throughout all four of my high school years, she took it upon herself to hand-make all my clothes. I'd peruse magazines for styles I wanted to try, and then she'd find the fabric and replicate them.

Before I got creative with my new clothes, I'd worn old hand-me-downs that people had given me. There wasn't anything particularly distinguishing about me. You wouldn't have called me a handsome kid. In fact, I hated to have my picture taken. When someone pulled out a camera, I'd run away until the threat was gone. Because of my rough-and-tumble go-kart spills, it wasn't uncommon to see Band-Aids all over my hands, arms, and legs.

But in my new threads, I looked nothing like my classmates. I'd show up to class wearing wild plaid bell-bottoms and big shirts with wide-open collars and long velvet sleeves. Each piece of clothing was customized, tailored specifically to me.

For a shy, unpopular teenager like me—a relatively skinny, mechanically minded introvert who had a couple of close friends but no girlfriend or social life to speak of—my wardrobe became an experiment, a personality test, you could say, that helped me analyze my classmates and distinguish friend from foe. My outward appearance was a reflection of my inner ambition, and I tried my best to look like a hippie, a real nonconformist. People either embraced my eccentric style, or they rejected it. Either way was fine by me.

In my high school, each student was assigned to one of several educational paths. Among them were the precollege level, which I envied, and the vocational level, which was designed for students who were preparing to go directly into the workforce after graduation. I belonged to the latter, having been placed in that track before my freshman year.

Eventually, and not without a lot of elbow grease, I earned my way into the college prep group. My heart was set on MIT, on the best degree from the best engineering school in the world. I kept this goal to myself, feeling too insecure to boast about it to anyone else, but that was my plan.

But my wallet said otherwise. I worked a few jobs in high school, furiously saving every penny of the three or four dollars I earned each week. By my senior year, however, it wasn't enough. I'd managed to scrounge up enough funds to cover the tuition costs of one semester in college. And that didn't include room and board.

My dream of studying at MIT was dwindling. Also, and this dismayed me greatly, I never heard back from them. I'd expected somebody from that great institution to respond to my handwritten letter, and when the mail came, I'd usually be the first to scour through it, searching in vain for my name, pining for that magic envelope.

For all my anticipation, I never received a reply. No one even acknowledged my passionate plea for admission.

The reason, which I later realized but didn't know at the time, was a careless mistake on my part. In the excitement of the moment, overwhelmed by the thrill of the article and the photos of the library and the thought of studying with some of the greatest minds in the world, I'd addressed the envelope to "New England," thinking it was like sending a Christmas list to Santa at the North Pole. Surely, I thought, the post office knew where MIT was.

I would never know what became of that letter, but I felt the absence of a response every single day. The rejection was palpable, the silence deafening. They were telling me I wasn't good enough, or smart enough, and that drove me crazy when I thought about it.

But it also drove me forward.

The longer I waited to hear back from MIT, the more resolved I became to solve this great problem before me. I became even more focused, more singular in my determination to end up in Cambridge. Even if my path required me to follow in my brothers' footsteps to Baldwin Wallace, eventually I'd find my way to MIT.

I'll show them, I told myself. *I'll show them that I belong there.*

5

STORMS

Ashtabula, Ohio
July 1965

A storm was brewing over the choppy waters of Lake Erie as I aimed the bow of my fifteen-foot sailboat into the heart of the squall.

Somewhere behind me, across the rolling waves and the rain that fell in sheets, was Ashtabula, about a mile from our current position. In clearer weather, the coast would have appeared like a thin line on the horizon. But now, amid the thrashing wind, the rolling seas, and the icy liquid bleeding into my wetsuit, there was only one thing I was looking for: the chill and thrill of adventure.

When I was about fourteen, and not yet old enough to drive, my father took me to buy my sailboat. It had been owned by a young man who was drafted into the Vietnam War a few months before, so it was almost brand new. She was a "Sailfish," little more than a heavy surfboard with a single sail and rudder, and she was worth every penny of the $125 I paid for her.

I built a trailer for my new boat so I could pull it to the beach with my bicycle—a three-speed, blue-and-chrome Schwinn Corvette. Once I unhitched it, I had to carry the Sailfish down a full set of stairs, across an eroded path, and through what must have been the largest infestation of rats in the entire town. Getting it into the water required finesse, to say the least. Getting it out of the water, though, especially after a long day of sailing, was truly a struggle.

But compared to my go-kart, the Sailfish was easy to operate. One hand controlled the sail, the other controlled the rudder. The ship was a pleasure to pilot, but for one major flaw. My boat had no heavy, fixed keel on the bottom of its hull to counter the force of the wind on the sail. If the crew—whether it be one, two, or at most, three of us—weren't careful in our positions, the whole thing could instantly flip and catapult us overboard. This happened only a few times before I borrowed a wetsuit from my brother, who was learning to scuba dive. If I'd be landing in frigid waters, at least I'd stay warm.

The Sailfish was designed for speed, not stability. And on a windy day when the waves were too turbulent for waterskiing, when even the fishing boat captains refused to leave the harbor, I'd take my friends out on the lake and open up the sail, and we'd have the time of our lives.

On days like this one, I kept my eyes to the skies, yearning for the perfect storm, waiting for the weather to turn sour, knowing full well that the fiercer the wind, the faster the speed.

You might say that I was born into something of a storm. My two older brothers viewed me as their guinea pig, and it was always two against one. Their pranks came in waves, one after the next,

Don Schoendorfer

and if their goal was to make my life uncomfortable, they achieved it in spades.

One afternoon, when I was about eight years old, my brothers hid my pet rabbit. In the rabbit's cage, they left a tableau of empty gun cartridges and spilled ketchup, designed to look like a bloody massacre. When I stumbled upon the grisly scene, I burst into tears and filled the house with shrieks of terror.

I followed the sound of raucous laughter, and there they were, the two of them, standing in the doorway, gasping for breath and delighting at my horror.

When I was a young child, I remember my father saying, "I don't want any more kids!"

"Yeah," my mother would respond, "but you're not in control." I don't think my life was an accident, but my brothers certainly told me it was.

My mother saw the toll these pranks were taking on me, and sometimes at night, before I fell asleep, she'd come up to my room, lie in bed with me, and say, "Your brothers are going to do great things, but you're going to do greater things." She'd tell me how smart I was, how I was a hard worker, and how my imagination would take me further than anyone could ever go.

It only happened a few times, but my mother's words of whispered affirmation kept something alive in me that otherwise might have died.

As a child, I did have a vivid imagination. When I was very young, my parents would come home sometimes to find a surprise waiting for them in the living room. While they were away, I'd converted the whole sofa into a full-sized boat, complete with an outboard motor made of books and blocks, and all the engine sounds you'd expect. I'd watch my mother survey the room, a slight smile on her face.

One year, to keep the three of us busy and out of trouble, my father ordered a kit for a sixteen-foot wooden boat. "Let's build a boat!" he announced. My brothers put more elbow grease into the project than I did, but I watched with rapt attention as the kit materialized, took shape, and eventually became a proper sailing vessel with a steering wheel and controls. My father lacquered the beautiful mahogany so it glistened, and he painted the hull a shiny black.

For a solid year, we worked on that boat in the garage and eventually named it the *Black Bomb*. After the boat was constructed, my father bought a new outboard motor and affixed it to the stern. He even managed to scrounge up enough money so we could join the local boat club, which gave us access to a dock on Lake Erie. There were some very expensive boats in the club, boats that dwarfed the *Black Bomb* in size and luxury. But our modest boat was big enough to fit our whole family, though we rarely went out on the lake together, all five of us.

On the roughest days, we'd take the *Black Bomb* out just for fun. To maneuver from the boat club to the lake, we had to pass through a treacherous channel no wider than a two-lane highway. Depending on how the wind was blowing, the waves could be barreling into the channel. We'd have to swallow our fear and strategize a way to avoid being thrown into the breakwall.

The motor was powerful enough to get us home, and just barely strong enough for water skiing. It was a real fight to get up out of the water as the boat struggled to reach her speed. But, as was the usual habit of our family, we made all sorts of improvements to the skis so they would have less drag. Still, you had to hang onto that rope like your life depended on it.

With my brothers, there were occasional moments of kindness. One day, they picked me up from school and offered to take me on a

Don Schoendorfer

ride on our little motorboat. I went with them reluctantly—on edge the whole time, certain that the real plan was to tie me to a buoy and leave me somewhere out on the lake. To my great relief, though, on that particular day they had decided simply to be kind.

But those days were few and far between. I spent much of my childhood on high alert, ready to absorb the next joke, the next punch. Still, my parents made sure we had a lot of fun growing up. There was never a shortage of freedom and latitude to explore, to design, to create, and to invent.

Once a month, all summer long, our boat club would host a fish fry. We'd be famished, standing in line for the fish, tempted by the delicious smell of hot oil and seasoned breading, and as people gathered behind us, my father would suddenly pull us out of line and lead us to the back of the line. He did this over and over again, a "last shall be first" kind of thing, which irritated me to no end.

In 1963, with my father's retirement on the horizon, he looked forward to spending more time with us on the boat. He hadn't quite worked fifty years, so to get the full pension he was due, the railroad allowed him to seek out employment that would add a few more years to his tally. He took a job as a crossing guard for the local elementary school, and after working half a century, my father was earning less than three dollars an hour. A few years later, I had a summer job as a laborer in road construction, and it struck me as tremendously sad that I was earning more per hour than my father had at the end of his long career as a machinist with the railroad.

But he made the most of his newly minted freedom. "Let's go fishing," he'd say to me, and I'd scramble to grab my rod and reel. At the time, Lake Erie was so polluted that we couldn't keep the fish we caught. We had to throw them back for someone else to catch and release. This didn't bother me much, though. I just enjoyed being out on the water with my dad, listening to the radio. Without all the interference on dry land, we'd pick up radio frequencies from Detroit and spend hours listening to the Supremes and the Temptations, to the new and different Motown stations we couldn't get at home.

We'd been on the choppy water for about an hour when the wind really picked up. I gave my friends a nod to make sure we were all in agreement. It was time to head for shore and have the wind to our backs. This was the fastest tack for a Sailfish, running with the waves and the wind.

I released the rope. We pulled our legs out of the water, and not a split second later, the three of us felt the burst of speed, the violent push forward propelled by the force of the wind. We held on as best we could.

We were now reaching speeds of more than twenty knots. We'd fly off the crest of one wave and plunge onto another, an exhilarating roller coaster of ups and downs, traveling across the water as fast as my go-kart could travel across land.

At first, the speed made steering difficult, and at last, it became impossible. The flip was inevitable, unavoidable. All three of us saw the large waving coming, rising up behind us and turning us over. Everything went blue, then we popped up out of the water, laughing with a rush of adrenaline.

We turned to make another run, this one farther from the shore and with higher waves. The waves were so high that when we were between them, in the trough, the horizon disappeared. A few minutes later, we saw a boat coming toward us. It was the Coast Guard. Their boats were the kind that can be tipped upside down and then right

Don Schoendorfer

themselves again—the kind made for rough weather. The treacherous waters of Lake Erie have sunk more than a few ships. The Coast Guard knows this and patrols the rough seas around Ashtabula, searching for vessels in distress.

"You boys are going to die out here!" one of the coasties shouted, trying to project his voice over the rush of the wind. The waves were crashing over my head, but I could see his bright-orange life vest. "You need to head back to shore right now!"

"Yes, sir," I shouted back. "We'll go right back, right now."

We turned to head downwind, right to the shore with the wind at our back, knowing the Coast Guard wouldn't be able to keep up. In less than a minute, we were out of sight.

It was probably foolhardy, but as soon as we were clear, we turned around and went right back out again. It was a calculated risk. Even if the boat broke in half, we knew we'd get home. With the onshore wind and our wetsuits, all we had to do was float and let the waves drift us slowly back to shore.

———

It would be decades before I understood how significant those waves of Lake Erie actually were. I didn't realize at the time that, as I drifted back to shore, yielding to the natural laws that governed the wind and the water, I was actually resting in the hands of a God who cared far more about my life than I knew.

As my brothers and I grew up, my parents made great efforts to involve us in the life of our church. But I never could find a way to connect with a God who seemed so distant and irrelevant to my life. Sure, maybe God had created the world—I was willing to give Him that—but I couldn't see any evidence that He'd been involved since.

I sat through church sermons, listening to a preacher who never seemed to have any problems of his own, while daydreaming about my Sailfish, counting down the seconds until I'd be back on the water again, riding the waves.

Back then, what I didn't know was that God's fingerprints were all over those waves. And one day, I'd realize they were covering me as well.

6

ZIGZAG

Berea, Ohio
July 1968

B ob Dylan was right about the 1960s.

The times, they were a-changing. And I had changed, too. I'd graduated from high school in 1967 with great grades, but my school wasn't on the level of those that would get me into MIT. So I'd decided to go ahead and complete my undergraduate liberal arts education at Baldwin Wallace before transferring to Columbia University to finish up my engineering degree.

During my first summer at Baldwin Wallace, I'd bought an old telephone repair van for only a hundred dollars. It seemed like a fair price for a vehicle with a couple hundred thousand miles of use. The van had once been a spacious workshop, with tools stashed on the wooden shelves that lined its walls. There was also ample space in the front because the engine was nestled between the driver and the passenger and functioned as a third seat because it was covered by a large piece of metal casing.

My neighbor and I spent the whole summer rebuilding that van, modifying it, making it roadworthy. He worked at a local Ford dealership. Whenever we needed a special tool, he'd just go to work and borrow it, which came in handy when we realized what a museum of problems that van turned out to be.

The thing leaked oil like it had a disease, a real hemorrhaging problem. From the mess it left on the driveway, you'd always know exactly where I'd parked it. Also, and this was a problem that needed immediate attention, the sides of the van were metal and rattled so violently on the road that your head would start to throb from the sound.

I had to find a way to make the interior more quiet, more bearable, so I bought large, gray swaths of thick carpet and glued the shaggy stuff everywhere—all over the floor, the dashboard, the sides, the roof. Then, to muffle the vibration even more, I found an old tube radio in our garage and installed it directly beneath the passenger's seat. The louder the rattling, the louder I'd crank that radio. My trip to New York City was going to be memorable, to say the least.

When September of 1970 arrived, it was time for me to go. I packed my bags, loaded them into the back of my loud, furry van, and said my goodbyes to friends, to family, and also to Lake Erie, whose coast had been a cradle to me since birth. I was now twenty years old and a student at Columbia, and I'd finally followed my dream all the way to New York City. With each passing mile, Ohio was disappearing in my rearview mirror.

I tapped the gas a little harder, speeding through the yellow light before it had a chance to blush at my van and me. I'd named my van *ZigZag*, partially after the popular French cigarette rolling paper, but mainly because the worn-out kingpins of the steering wheel forced me to turn the wheel about a third of a turn before the van would change course. My van required full concentration to keep from zigzagging down the road.

It was a sight, that van. But how could I have known, when painting it dark gray back in Ohio, that I was making it virtually invisible to the cars that kept hitting it in the dorm's parking lot? Now, some two months later, the *ZigZag* was all dinged and dented. People just kept backing into it.

To remedy this oversight, I decided that my van needed some color, some bright cartoon characters. I painted a very clumsy Goofy on the front and five of Snow White's seven dwarves on the driver's side. For the back of the vehicle, which suffered most of the damage, I reserved a special character taken from one of my favorite films, *Yellow Submarine.* His name was "Jeremy Hillary Boob, PhD," a pudgy, eccentric scientist with a bright-blue face and brown fur all over his body.

And wouldn't you know it? Not long after my paint job, my van stopped getting sideswiped, though it certainly turned more than a few heads when I pulled it onto campus.

The move had been a big change for this small-town boy from Ashtabula, but like everybody else in my class, I was adjusting to life in New York City. At Columbia, I always found myself in a hurry, and this day was no exception. I had a very important meeting, and nothing was going to slow me down, especially not red lights. Not today. Not on *this* particular morning.

With the Hudson River on my left and Central Park up on the right, I drove through the theater district on Broadway, one of my newly discovered favorite slices of the Big Apple.

In the first few decades of the nineteenth century, and certainly at the height of the roaring twenties, folks used to call this stretch of Broadway "The Great White Way," nicknamed for its dazzling lights. Those were the glory years of American entertainment and industry, the golden age for wealthy tycoons like Rockefeller, Carnegie, Gould, and Morgan—those titans who moved humanity forward with their brilliant ideas and clever inventions.

I wanted to follow in their footsteps, to share their visions. Their optimism inspired me. Their ambition was rubbing off on me, even if I didn't know exactly how to pick up where they'd left off. Were there any new technologies waiting for me to discover? There had to be, but none came to mind.

Perhaps I'd need to combine technologies that already existed to create something original. That's what Wilbur and Orville Wright did in their bicycle shop in Dayton, Ohio, only a few hours from my home in Ashtabula. Those aviation pioneers came up with a brilliant idea: to add wings to wheels. In 1903, this idea resulted in the invention of the *Wright Flyer*, the first aircraft capable of controlled, sustained, engine-powered flight. I loved the legacy of those two brothers, and also the legacy that Henry Ford left. It was easy to see why so many looked up to them.

As for me, I had no clue what my legacy would look like. But as I drove beneath the looming skyscrapers on Broadway, weaving through traffic and dodging taxis, I did know one thing. I knew that some great purpose had brought me to this city, to this land of giants. Call it destiny, if you'd like. I felt that a certain destiny was calling me, something bigger than me, more important than me.

What exactly that was, I could not say, and it would be years before I recognized it as God's guidance in my life. But I couldn't deny it, that feeling of excitement when I thought about what was waiting for me on the other side of my education. Whatever it was,

Don Schoendorfer

I knew I had to meet it with all my strength. Whatever the venture, or adventure, I was determined to make my talents equal to my task, even if I didn't have the money to afford it.

In my last year at Baldwin Wallace, I'd received a modest scholarship from Columbia. They were going to cover 50 percent of my tuition costs. Not bad, really. I could use every penny they'd give me. But this still left me with a large deficit that I had to find a way to fill. The money I'd earned as a paperboy and in four years' worth of summer work as a laborer on a road construction crew wasn't going to cover my expenses, not with the extra cost of living in New York City.

But I knew I had to survive because my future depended on it. An engineering degree from Columbia was essential, a necessary stepping-stone on the way to achieving my ultimate goal: a PhD from MIT.

One anxious afternoon, a couple of weeks after I'd settled in at Columbia, as I sat worrying about how I was going to afford my education, a letter arrived in my box. Most of my mail sat unopened for weeks, forgotten as I memorized endless lists of equations. But this one was different. I ripped open the envelope.

The letter was from the dean of Columbia's engineering department. I skimmed the introduction until my eyes absorbed the glowing, glorious message.

Columbia is going to pay for every bit of my tuition!

I could hardly believe my luck. The university was going to pay for *all of it*. The timing couldn't have been better. But when I decided to read the rest of the letter, I sobered up in a hurry.

There was a catch.

In exchange for covering all of my expenses, the dean requested that I meet the benefactors of my scholarship face to face. Something inside me started to panic. The luncheon would be organized by the Columbia University Alumni Association. My eyes went back to that word, *benefactors*. A flood of doubts started to gnaw away at me. *What if they don't like me?*

I was grateful for their gift, but I dreaded meeting them. The very thought of that luncheon haunted me. It conjured up all of my oldest fears and insecurities. *I don't even own clothes nice enough to meet "benefactors."*

This is how I imagined the meeting would go:

I'd show up with my cartoon van at some fancy dining room, all crystal and cloth, and everyone would see that I'd have no business being there. The wealthy benefactors would introduce themselves, they'd take a look at me with knowing eyes, and then the whole meal would be awkward and filled with pitiful glances in my direction. I'd watch them watching me, studying me, determining whether or not I was worthy of their money, their time. *What if they withdraw the offer?*

My life in New York became filled with those questions, those "what ifs." *What if I'm not good enough? What if I'm not smart enough?*

My mother once asked me what I wanted to do with my life. On some level, I knew she hoped that I'd be a financial success, and Uncle George's wealth always did interest me, but I never heard him talk much about money. He never complained about having to pay bills or make ends meet. For my uncle, the ends always seemed to meet.

I knew that earning a PhD in higher education would increase my chances of gaining the same kind of freedom that Uncle George enjoyed. I wanted to be independent, to avoid a life of working on the assembly line. I didn't want to take orders from anybody. I didn't want to work for a boss. I was much more attracted to the idea of being a visionary, the one who figured out the mechanics of an idea and assembled the pieces like a jigsaw puzzle.

Making money for money's sake wasn't my uncle's greatest desire, and it wasn't mine, either. Some of my friends at Columbia talked a lot about it, though. They dreamed of earning vast fortunes from their inventions. And they weren't just talking millions, either. They were talking *billions*.

To me, though, the very idea of selling a product for a profit, the idea of commercialization, just didn't make any sense. *Why wouldn't you sell something for what it costs?* I'd understand taking 10 percent off the top, just to cover living expenses. That seemed reasonable enough. But *billions*?

The only thing I ever wanted to do was to get the best education I could. Then I'd be able to do something good for the world. Maybe even something *great*.

One day, months after I had met with the benefactors who funded my scholarship—a luncheon that went surprisingly well, to my great relief—I was walking back to school along Broadway, just about to cross the busy street onto Columbia's campus. It was a sprawling, urban campus. The whole area occupied more than six blocks of Morningside Heights, the turbulent neighborhood of Upper West Side Manhattan.

As the sun warmed my back, a welcome change from the frosty nip of winter, I was reflecting on my progress so far. At Columbia, I was surrounded by geniuses, Nobel Prize winners—physicists and chemists who possessed remarkable natural aptitude. I was constantly competing against people who were much more intelligent than I was.

From the perspective of grades, I had proven myself well enough. I was actually a great student, even though none of it came easily to me. I had to work ten times harder than my peers for every single "A."

Soon, it would be time for all of us to narrow in on our specific areas of concentration. Some of my peers would accept jobs at impressive corporations. Others would continue on to graduate school. Either way, it was time to hone our focus. We had to decide on what aspect of engineering excited us most, what particular field we'd spend the rest of our lives dedicated to.

Most of my friends were talking about Texas Instruments or the aerospace and automotive industries. Those were the three big hires.

But to me, those giants had no appeal. If I went with any of them, I'd just be grouped with a lot of other people who were all working to solve one big problem. And for what purpose? To make a better car or a better computer? To help a large company become even richer? It made more sense to me for products to be sold at cost, or nearly at cost. And besides, I wanted to do something new, something that had never been done before.

I stepped off the curb and into the crosswalk. Then, out of nowhere, it hit me.

What if there were a way to combine engineering with something else? The notion had come out of the blue and struck me like a bolt of white lightning, followed by a clap of loud thunder. *That's how I could really help people. What if I combine mechanical engineering and medicine?*

The thought stopped me dead in my tracks, in the middle of Broadway. I was so stunned by the revelation that I couldn't even move. At long last, I had found something exciting to latch on to, a way to truly help people, to make a real difference in other people's lives. Engineers had been helping doctors for decades, but I'd never thought of it as a possibility for me.

All of a sudden, I heard the sound of the traffic all around me, a cacophony of noise snapping me back to reality. I caught the angry glare of a delivery driver who was bearing down hard on his horn.

A man in a shiny sedan leaned out of his window, shaking his fist at me. "Get out of the way, you stupid idiot!" he yelled.

I stumbled out of my stupor and scurried across the street. But this time, unlike all the other times I had walked onto that campus, there was something different. In that moment, I'd become a new kind of man with a new kind of mission. I had a very specific vision, a daring dream that MIT was going to make come true. The pieces of my life had finally started to fall into place. I knew what I had to do.

I didn't need to reinvent the wheel. All I needed to do was spin it in a new direction.

7

LAURIE

New York City
December 1971

F all gave way to winter, and winter succumbed to spring. I was
in my second year at Columbia. Not that I noticed. I spent
nearly every waking moment with my nose buried deep in
some book, studying relentlessly. Just like in middle and high school,
I'd made a few close friends but kept mostly to myself.

I avoided people as best I could and always found great satisfaction working alone instead of in a group. The group projects, which were ubiquitous at Columbia, just weren't my thing. They never suited me. We'd break into groups of four, and I'd always be the quiet one who went along with whatever the group wanted to do, probably because I hated confrontation.

One evening, after seeing that I hadn't come up for air in weeks, a buddy of mine invited me to a party at his girlfriend's place. I needed a break, no doubt about it, and decided to tag along.

As we walked into the apartment, my eyes skimmed the room, sizing everyone up, taking in the flood of laughter. We brushed by a crowd of conversations and over to my buddy's girlfriend, whom he wanted me to meet. But as he was making introductions, it was the woman standing beside her who captured my attention.

"Don Schoendorfer," I said, extending my hand to the beautiful woman with the strawberry-blonde hair.

She took it. "Laurie Graham," she replied, her eyes squinting into a wide, easy smile. I tried not to be too bothered by the young man at her side. *Her boyfriend?* He slid his arm around the small of her waist, and my eyes followed.

As the evening progressed, I succeeded at making casual conversation with her. I learned that she'd been a theology student at Mount Holyoke College in Massachusetts before moving to New York City to work with the Social Security Administration. She was eloquent and obviously very intelligent. I was amazed by the way her mind worked, by the way she processed questions. I wanted to know more, to hear her talk about music and politics and everything in between. I hadn't dated many women at all, but I knew that there was something special about this one. I'd never met anyone like Laurie Graham, and I was smitten.

Turned out the guy *was* Laurie's boyfriend. And when he left the party, I felt that my opportunity had arrived. I had to seize the moment before I lost the nerve.

"Laurie," I said, feeling unsure of myself, "I don't want to overstep . . ." She looked at me like she might have known what I was going to ask. "But if you'd be interested," I continued, "I'd like to take you on a date sometime."

———————

Over the weeks that followed, I fell hard for Laurie. What she saw in me, however, I'll never really know.

I didn't think of myself as handsome, even though I was in pretty decent shape. Compared to the other men in her life, I was fairly crude and rough around the edges. With my wacky van and big ideas, I was easily the weirdest guy she'd ever dated.

Laurie was already a professional woman, out in the workforce and earning a living. I, on the other hand, had a long road of education still stretching out ahead of me. I wanted the best degree from the best school in the world, and even though I didn't know what the outcome would be, I hoped that MIT was my future.

Also, Laurie's Catholic faith was central to her life. By this time, my religion didn't surface at all. Sure, I gave God credit for creating the universe, but it wasn't like I would pray, and I definitely had no desire to go to church.

On top of all that, at the very beginning of our relationship, I'd brashly presented Laurie with a fairly unappealing offer. During that season, Laurie's roommate, and some of her other friends, had all become engaged to be married. I knew that marriage wouldn't work for me right then. I was trying to sustain a single-minded focus, so I had to be clear.

"Laurie," I said, "I don't want to waste anybody's time, and I really feel bad when people waste mine."

She looked at me quizzically.

"I've got to come clean with you," I said. "The three most important things in my life are a PhD, a PhD, and a PhD. And that's what I'm going to do."

Laurie sat in silence as I continued. "And you're welcome to be my girlfriend, and I'd be happy to have you be my girlfriend, but you've got to know that's what I'm doing. So, if we develop a relationship, Laurie, you just have to understand this about me. And I can't change this; it's how I'm wired. I'm programmed to be this way. I love you, and I love this relationship with you, but I need to study. I need to work."

I held my breath for a few seconds as she processed the weight of my words. Then, to my great surprise, Laurie began to nod. As it turned out, she found it refreshing for a man to be so up front with his intentions.

"All right," she agreed. "Let's do it."

8

MADE IT

New York City
March 1972

As it turned out, there was a limit to the lengths to which my mother would go to support my fashion choices.

"Donnie," she said, shaking her head with resolve, "you're going too far."

My years at Columbia had come to an end, and with my new plan to focus on biomedical engineering for my doctoral work at MIT, I'd crammed in as much science as I could manage, filling every elective and then some. Biochemistry, physics, biology, chemistry—I took every class, knowing that I'd need an impressive array of prerequisites on my resume to attract the attention of the famed MIT engineering department.

All my hard work finally paid off when I received the invitation to interview for a spot in the program. I was confident that my van could transport me safely on the two-hundred-mile drive from New York City to Cambridge, Massachusetts, the quirky enclave of metropolitan Boston that was home to both MIT and Harvard—two institutions that were as different as night and day.

I knew of Harvard's reputation, of its conservatively dressed students who were almost uniformed, similar to what I'd seen at Columbia. But I needed to know that MIT would be a different sort of place, a place packed with liberal thinkers who were open to new ideas. I needed to know that MIT was a place where people wouldn't be judged by their appearance, where I, with my own abundance of quirkiness, could fit in.

I'd spent my whole adolescence studying reactions to my non-conformist clothing, a useful litmus test for reading people quickly. So, on the one hand, I was fully aware of the opportunity before me, that I was being interviewed by my dream school. But on the other hand, I was determined to conduct an interview of my own. My wardrobe had not failed me in the past, and I was confident it would come through for me in the future.

When the morning arrived, I gave myself one last look in the mirror. Several years earlier, my mother, thinking I'd ventured beyond the pale of appropriate attire, had been unwilling to indulge my need for a wool cape. So I'd turned to a friend to sew what had now become the crown jewel of my outrageous interview outfit. Even Laurie tried hard to avoid thinking about my oddball scheme, having caught a glimpse of my clothes before she kissed me goodbye and wished me luck.

And what an outfit it was! The wool cape was herringbone gray with a black velvet lining. It went to my knees and had slits in the sides for me to slip my hands into. A frog and tassel closure kept it snugly secured around my shoulders. Under the cape, I wore a pair of broad plaid bell-bottoms and boots, since it was winter. And of course, the icing on the cake, the pièce de résistance, was a collapsible top hat that sat tall and proud on the crown of my head.

Even in free-spirited Cambridge, where every day was Halloween, no one ever wore top hats.

With my cape donned, I turned away from the mirror, walked by the couch where my friend had let me sleep, poured a cup of hot coffee with milk and sugar, and then slipped out of the apartment.

I pulled my cartooned van into MIT, startled by the size of the campus. It was as huge as I'd imagined, just as sprawling and spacious as it was on the brochure I'd saved all those years. I immediately saw the dome of the engineering school's library rising high above the two-story building. It looked just like it had in the photo, only taller and wider. The engineering department, being the first school on the campus, was among the oldest collection of buildings at MIT, innovative and full of personality.

I parked my van and walked into the dark, stuffy building, my cape flying behind me as I climbed up the worn-out stairs. *Sure doesn't smell like an innovative place*, I thought. *Smells like an old library.* When I arrived on the second floor, I removed my top hat, collapsed it, and walked into the office.

"Don Schoendorfer," I said to the secretary. She didn't bat a single eyelash at my cape. *A promising start.* Then she ushered me into the office of Professor Shapiro, the department chair and a man whom I'd long admired. He'd written a foundational book on compressible fluid dynamics that I'd studied at Columbia, and he was a pioneer in the burgeoning field of biomedical engineering. Professor Shapiro was a legend at MIT and meeting him face-to-face was a dream come true.

As I waited for him to arrive, I sized up the room. In front of me was a large desk covered with stacks of books and scattered papers, and on a nearby table, a few engineering magazines and an open box of cigars. I got the feeling that this was the office of someone who did serious work—a working office, not a show office.

"I hear you're considering MIT," Professor Shapiro said, walking into the room, getting right to the point. I stood to shake his hand.

"Yes sir," I said. "Coming to MIT has been my life's dream."

He looked at me briefly, then turned his attention to the file on the desk. With each passing second, as his eyes skimmed my transcript, I wondered if I'd done enough, if I'd taken enough science electives to earn merit with MIT.

"Your academic record is sterling," he finally said, to my great relief. "What do you want to study?"

"I'd really like to study biomedical engineering. It's an exciting new field, and I think I could make a real contribution there."

"Biomedical engineering," he said. "If you're interested in that, you might find some good projects to work on here." He described some of the work going on in the engineering department, like the exciting new effort to develop innovative technologies for artificial shoulders, elbows, and knees. I hung on his every word.

Within minutes, the interview was over, and the secretary was showing me out of his office. I punched open my top hat and bounced down the staircase and out of the building, a childlike giddiness in each step. My dream had finally come true, the one conceived on that fateful day in my parents' kitchen when I first saw MIT's advertisement. All my hard work and late nights of studying had just paid off, in a matter of minutes. And my cape and outfit, they hadn't garnered so much as a second glance. I knew MIT was a place where I could think outside the box. The whole morning had been a massive success.

I sprinted across the parking lot and toward my van, exhilarated by the final words of the interview, words that sounded like a majestic symphony playing on repeat in my mind:

"Mr. Schoendorfer, I think you're going to do very well here."

9

EASY RIDER

New York City
June 1972

T o my great surprise and even greater relief, MIT ended up
offering me a full scholarship. Tuition, room, board, and
even a stipend—the institution covered every bit of it.

The occasion called for celebration, so I decided to spend the
summer exploring Europe by motorcycle, a victory lap of sorts. I
eventually managed to convince Laurie to join me, but it wasn't easy.
In my mind, I was offering Laurie a pretty good deal—a vacation
for eleven weeks on the back of a motorcycle, airfare not included.

Laurie knew I was committed to my educational trajectory, and
that after the summer I'd be settling in Boston for at least the next four
years, but she fought saying yes to my offer for months. Why would
she quit her job to spend the summer on a motorcycle with a guy
she'd only known for a few months? Then one day, out of the blue, I
could tell that she'd changed her mind, but in true Laurie fashion, she
wasn't going to admit it easily. We made a trivial bet on the volume of a
Chemex coffee pot, and when I won, she agreed to join me in Europe.

There was, of course, one condition. We couldn't let her parents find out. They'd go ballistic if they knew she was heading to Europe to ride a motorcycle with this weirdo.

I arrived early at JFK and hid behind a Coca-Cola machine at the gate of departure, because Laurie was certain her parents would show up, take one look at me, and drag her back home. When they didn't, and I was sure the coast was clear, we darted onto the plane, excited for the journey of a lifetime to begin.

Laurie and I spent three blissful months traveling from one country to another, camping our way across the continent. We lived on a couple of dollars a day and showered only twice a week. By the time we returned from that unforgettable summer, Laurie had decided to follow me back to Boston, where she secured a job with the Social Security Administration.

We later took that same motorcycle on another unforgettable drive through New England in the summer of 1974, one of a hundred we'd make over the years to come. Just as we entered the ferry that would transport us from Long Island, New York, to Providence, Rhode Island, a storm rolled in. The waves grew violent on the water, tossing the front of the ferry up and down as passengers boarded. Sheets of rain pelted the roof of the cabin where Laurie and I were huddled. It reminded me of Lake Erie and the thrill I'd once felt as a young, wave-chasing teenager going out in my Sailfish.

A woman walked into the passenger cabin wearing not one, but *two* life jackets. She was prepared for the worst. "This is going to be a rough trip!" Laurie said, her eyes wide. Then, totally out of the blue, her voice took a serious tone. "What if you don't want to get married? What if I've spent five years of my life—a good part of my life—with a guy that doesn't want to get married?"

Don Schoendorfer

For a moment, I was stunned into silence, couldn't get a word out. Laurie was right. I'd been on autopilot without giving thought to the future, to *our* future.

"You're absolutely right," I finally said. "I'm so sorry for not thinking about this from your perspective. Let's get married!"

So we did. Three weeks later, at her family's summer house in Connecticut, in the presence of our families and a couple dozen friends, Laurie was standing beside me in a perfectly fitting wedding dress she found on sale for twenty-five dollars. We knew we didn't have much, but that was okay. We had each other. And that was all that really mattered.

In my early days at MIT, I explored some of the projects in the mechanical engineering department that Professor Shapiro had mentioned in my interview. I familiarized myself with the artificial knee and elbow projects, and with the burgeoning telemedicine field. But in the end, those initiatives turned out to be little more than big groups of people working on little pieces of larger projects, which had no appeal for me. The PhD students working on those projects were required to sit in tiny bullpens, not even large enough to be considered cubicles, and they all had to share a machine shop. I knew myself well enough to know that as a creative introvert I wouldn't thrive working with groups of other people like that, especially groups of other engineers.

I explained my frustrations to Professor Shapiro, who suggested I look at some other departments. After nosing around a bit, investigating the different projects taking shape, I eventually made my way to Professor Jerome Lettvin, a brilliant Renaissance man who was a psychologist and rabbi with several PhDs and dual appointments in the departments of electrical engineering and biology. When I met some of his students, I knew I'd found a match made in heaven. They struck me as a bit off-the-wall, which was absolutely perfect, and the unconventional way they were tackling their projects fascinated me.

I scheduled an appointment with Professor Lettvin's secretary, and a few days later I made my way to his office. It was housed in an old Quonset hut, a half-cylinder, corrugated metal structure that the US Army had built to house MIT's accelerated program to develop radar for the war effort during World War II. Professor Lettvin's secretary was a gray-haired woman in her late fifties named Susan.

I walked over to the small desk where she was sitting and said, "Good afternoon. I have a two o'clock appointment with Professor Lettvin."

"He's indisposed at this time," Susan said.

From where I was standing, I could see directly into Professor Lettvin's office. And sure enough, to my surprise, there he was, lying down on the couch, snoring loudly.

"Okay, when can I come back?"

Susan lifted her eyes to meet mine. "Maybe tomorrow," she said, unenthusiastically.

The next day, I returned to his office to try to speak to the professor. I was becoming increasingly more anxious because I didn't yet have a thesis topic. When I arrived, I saw Professor Lettvin once again asleep, his secretary doing her best to ignore his snoring. She sent me away with instructions to return the next day, which I did. Then, as my third unsuccessful attempt gave way to a fourth, Susan offered me some helpful advice. "It might be best to talk to his assistant professor," she said.

Don Schoendorfer

Thankfully, I found Professor Raymond, his assistant professor, wide awake in his office. After I introduced myself, he asked me what I wanted to work on.

"I don't have a clue," I admitted. "But time is running out. I've only got a few months to come up with something."

Dr. Raymond seemed to mull over a few possibilities, then he said, "Well, I know of somebody who can't speak because he had a laryngectomy. Why don't you explore that field? Go figure out how many people have had their larynxes removed and then see what other people are doing to restore their speech."

I didn't know anything about sound, or acoustics, and I'd never met anyone who'd undergone a laryngectomy. But the idea of restoring sound to those who couldn't speak struck my curiosity, so I took his advice and got to work studying the physiology of the larynx.

The research was exciting. It caused me to think deeply about the plight of those who couldn't speak, the suffering and frustration of not having a voice—a disability that affected several hundred thousand people.

Muteness, as I learned, was caused most often by cancer surgery or by car accidents in which the victim's throat smashed into the steering wheel. I listened to those who were mute as they tried to speak. And beyond that, removing a person's larynx also affects the sense of smell, which hampers the ability to taste.

So, as I was making progress on my thesis, I was encountering those who had experienced traumatic loss in their life. Not only had they suffered the loss of the ability to communicate with their voices, which affects personality and identity, but they also suffered the loss of three of their five senses.

Thus far, science and technology had failed to invent an adequate solution to this problem, and to my knowledge no one else was even working on one. I was virtually alone in the quest to improve the quality of their lives.

It was a perfect fit for me, a wide-open lane in which to stretch my legs. My thesis became a way for me to be a voice for the voiceless, a way to restore the humanity and dignity that had been taken from so many people. I knew that if I truly dedicated myself to working the problem, perhaps I could do even more. Perhaps I could give them a voice of their own.

———————

There was plenty of room in Professor Lettvin's department for my thinking to stretch out and grow, but as it turned out, there wasn't any room for me to have an office.

"We don't have any space for you here," Professor Raymond said, "but there is a room in the biology department. You should take a look at it."

Following his advice, I went to the biology building, climbed a set of stairs, and discovered the space he was referring to. It was hardly an office at all, just an old storage room filled with junk, or so it seemed. When I looked more closely, I realized that the "junk" was abandoned equipment from the department's machine shop.

I could feel my heart begin to race as I explored the various machines and tools that lined the walls and filled the space, machines that had not been used in years but probably still worked. I'd never had access to equipment like this in all my life.

I had to find a pay phone.

"Dad!" I exclaimed into the receiver. "You won't believe it!"

As I shared the litany of machines that adorned my new office, I could hear his excitement on the other end of the phone.

"There's an old Bridgeport milling machine," I said, "and a South Bend lathe, and a . . ."

"Wait, you've got a South Bend lathe?" he interrupted. "Are you kidding me? You know, Donnie, I learned how to do machining for the first time on that very lathe! I can't wait to come visit!"

I couldn't believe my luck. Professor Raymond had provided me with the perfect thesis topic, and he'd also given me a treasure map that led to a dream office, a top-notch machinist laboratory, the envy of any doctoral student.

But there was work to do. I went back to the office and began clearing out the old fixtures, the hardware, the wiring and cages, and all sorts of other abandoned materials that had been used in past neurological investigations, things people didn't have a use for anymore but didn't want to throw away. I oiled up the lathe and the milling machine and set them up prominently in the room. But I would need some assistance getting them up and running.

Then, as if the entire universe were conspiring to help me succeed, I struck up a conversation with one of my new colleagues.

"You know they are moving Professor Lettvin and Professor Raymond's group into the brand new Electrical Engineering Building. This means you are allowed access to the research resources in the basement of this new building."

"What resources?" I asked.

"There's a machine shop down in the basement, and you can use it anytime. It's one of the perks of working in this building."

I went down to the basement of the department and found a fully operational machine shop, just like my colleague said. It had machines I'd never even seen before, and it was staffed by some of the most talented prototype machinists in the world. To my astonishment, and because MIT stressed that we had to understand what it takes to make things before we started designing things for other people to make, the staff in the basement would create anything the doctoral students needed or wanted. All we had to do was ask. I told them about the old milling machine and lathe in my office, and they generously helped me restore them to working condition. The staff became my tutors, and I became their apprentice.

"I've got to cut this machine bit for the lathe," I'd say to them, and then they'd show me how to do it correctly. When I'd bring the prototype back for their inspection, they'd offer kind and helpful feedback, saying, "No, you don't have it quite right. There's a little more of an angle here. And you've got to make sure you put this piece on tight because it can fly out like a knife."

As the ideas in my thesis materialized, and as I began experimenting with devices that could offer the ability to communicate to those who couldn't speak, I went down to that basement every chance I got. They helped me learn new skills and fine-tune my prototypes. Down there, surrounded by creative people who thought outside the box, who *dreamed* outside the box, I felt like a little boy again, and it was Christmas, and I had just unwrapped my very first Erector Set.

10

PATIENTS
AND PATENTS

Cambridge, Massachusetts
October 1974

Two years into my studies at MIT, I began preparing for my qualifying exam: a series of tests that would determine whether or not I'd be able to continue working toward my PhD. It was an intimidating test, one that every doctoral student feared, an obstacle that each of us had to hurdle.

To prepare, I needed to demonstrate mastery over four subjects: strength of materials, control theory, thermodynamics, and fluid mechanics. Problem was, I'd never even taken a single course on control theory. I purchased and read *Schaum's Outlines*, a condensed overview of the material, similar to CliffsNotes. The qualifying exam would include both written and oral parts, and I was nervous, to say the least. If I didn't pass this exam, my dream of a PhD would disappear. I'd even heard of students at MIT who had ended their lives after failing this exam.

When the morning of the written exams came, I was sweating bullets, staring down at questions on the paper, my mind scrambling to recall everything I'd memorized, my hands shaky. Soon after I began, I knew things weren't going well.

The oral part of the exam was next, and it was an embarrassment. For this final step of the process, each candidate's thesis committee would convene, weigh the circumstances, and decide whether we passed or failed. Professor Raymond was on my committee, along with three distinguished professors. My thesis work on laryngectomy patients was coming along swimmingly, and I was confident about my proficiency in that part, but I was a wreck trying to answer their questions.

"If you flip a coin," one of the professors asked me, "is it possible to have the coin rotate around all three axes so that you only see the head and not the tail?"

I began to visualize the simulation in my mind.

"Please provide the equations you need to prove your answer," he said.

I stumbled over my answer and also the next one. They tried to give me clues, one after another, but nothing helped. Eventually, I left the exam, utterly devastated and quite sure I had failed.

"It's not the end of the world," Laurie tried to tell me. But it sure felt like it.

A few terrifying weeks later, Professor Raymond asked me to come to his office. He told me that after I left the room, he had gone to bat for me.

"Listen," he told the other professors, "I don't know anything about mechanical engineering. I'm a professor of biology. But I can tell you that what Don is doing with his thesis is revolutionary and unusual and groundbreaking." Eventually, and after some deliberation on their part, Professor Raymond convinced the committee to give me a second chance.

"Don," they told me, "you couldn't have done much worse on your qualifying exam, but we've decided to give you another chance. You've got a year to prepare for it."

I was beside myself with fear and excitement. *Another year,* I thought. *I'm going to make it count.* Not only did I spend the next twelve months taking the four courses over again, for an entire year I studied exclusively for one test.

Sleeping took a back seat to studying, and so did everything else. I still had my thesis to work on, but I spent every spare minute studying for the qualifying exam, repeating the questions from the first exam over and over in my mind, figuring out how a flipped coin could rotate on all three axes with only its head facing in my direction and all the while knowing there'd be a host of new questions I hadn't anticipated. I'd go to my quiet office space early each morning, spend the whole day thinking and studying and preparing, and then return home late each night.

Weekends dissolved into weekdays. All day Sunday was given to my work. For an entire year, Laurie put up with seeing me for half a day on Saturday. To keep herself from getting bored, she decided to redeem the time by earning a master's degree in public administration.

Finally, the week of my do-over exam arrived. "Ask me anything!" I challenged Laurie. "I know it all!"

I walked into the oral exam, ready to answer questions I knew and questions I'd never even considered before.

The first question: "People mention that when they walk out onto the Golden Gate Bridge, they can hear humming. Could you please explain where that sound is coming from?"

I thought for a moment, then said, "When the wind goes over a cable at a certain speed, it produces vortices that break loose. At the right wind speed, these vortices can match the harmonic frequency of the cables, thus producing a resonance which, if it's within the audible frequency of the human ear, could cause this humming sound."

For a moment, my mind wandered back to my hometown. I thought of the Ashtabula bridge and the devastation that resulted from poor construction.

"And actually," I continued, "if this problem isn't resolved, these vortices can cause vibrations that could eventually destroy the cables. When engineers are designing bridges, they have to know how to reduce the impact of these forces on their construction."

The committee seemed pleased with my answer. "Please tell us the equations that you could use to avoid that," the professor said. "If I gave you the dimensions of the cable and the wind speed, could you determine what the frequency would be?"

Yes, this year I could do that. Even though I hadn't solved this question before, I was able to derive the equations. The method, the process, the way to determine the exact number—I found a way to come up with all of them. I started off with something simple, like Newton's Law (force is equal to mass times acceleration). Then, once I'd established the principles of that equation, I figured out the equations and formulas of other dynamics, such as velocity and pressure.

"Wait a minute, sir," the chairman interrupted. His eyes widened appreciatively. "We don't usually see students going back to the first principles like you're doing," he said. "So, if the bridge fell down, how would you, as a consultant, solve the problem that the other engineer failed to do?"

By the time I was done answering every line of questioning from the committee members, my hands were covered in white chalk and the blackboard behind me, the one I'd been writing on, was filled with equations, drawings, and solutions.

Never in all my life have I felt so smart. And as it turned out, I passed the examination. Even though it took an additional year, I'd overcome the greatest obstacle of my professional life and could continue with my PhD. From that day onward, everything felt possible and achievable. It was like a light bulb had suddenly flickered on in my mind, illuminating future projects, future possibilities.

Laurie and I celebrated the occasion by going out to dinner. And when I got home, I turned off the lights, fell into bed, and slept for what felt like a week.

———————

Five long years of hard work had finally paid off. I'd solved the problem that my thesis had identified: how to synthesize artificial speech for those who were about to lose their vocal cords.

Before a patient's laryngectomy procedure, I made a recording of his or her speech. Then, to simulate her pitch and intonation, I used a simple model of the human vocal cords with a miniature, breath-powered vibrating reed, much like the duck call I'd had as a child. After the patient healed, the surgeon inserted the miniature vibrating reed through a skin fistula leading to the base of the vocal track.

The invention actually worked! Not only was the prototype successful, but it could lead to radical changes in the lives of those who could no longer communicate. It would take a tremendous amount of work to perfect, but I believed I had proven the concept.

My PhD committee informed me that I was reaching the end of my studies and that MIT wanted to patent my discovery. But before I could graduate, I still needed to complete my PhD defense, a grueling examination that would test every aspect of my work.

Professor Lettvin, Professor Raymond, other members of my thesis committee, and Laurie were all present for my defense, along with a few dozen professors from various departments at MIT. They were all watching me as I pulled out my slides and began the presentation.

I explained how I'd come up with the artificial vocal cord, how I'd measured the activity of real vocal cords, and how those natural vocal cords are compromised because of the surgery. I had brought one of my prototypes with me to the defense and blew hard into the device, showing the committee the artificial throats that I'd created for different vowels. I connected the miniature artificial vocal cord prosthesis to the vocal track models and showed how the prosthesis was able to generate easily identified vowel sounds. Then, I played some tape recordings I'd taken from patients as they spoke their first words after their laryngectomies.

"Mr. Schoendorfer," one of the professors began, "do you actually have any statistics to prove that naïve listeners can understand these patients' speech?"

"Well," I fumbled, "I don't really have any . . ."

At that moment, and before I could get out the rest of my sentence, Professor Lettvin raised his hand. "Professor," he said, "you need statistics when you do not have a fact."

I shot a bewildered glance over at Laurie, who was just as surprised by the comment as everyone else in the room. Professor Lettvin continued, "We can clearly hear the person's voice before the operation, and we can clearly hear the person's voice after the operation, and that's a fact!"

Professor Lettvin's words carried a lot of weight. He was a trailblazer in his field, a neurophysiologist considered one of the most brilliant scientists at MIT. His groundbreaking discoveries in the spinal cord and retina, and his 1959 paper, "What the Frog's Eye Tells the Frog's Brain," brought him international recognition, as did his public debates with Timothy Leary, the controversial Harvard professor who encouraged the use of LSD.

Students adored him. He was unconventional and a bit disheveled, a charismatic professor whose reputation preceded him. Professor Lettvin didn't care what people thought about him, which I respected. And his philosophy—the greater the risk, the greater the discovery—led him to conduct unusual experiments. He believed that every human patient or laboratory animal must be fully restored to a comfortable life.

And I, being the test subject of the day, was no exception. Professor Lettvin's words, merciful and timely, convinced the entire committee of the legitimacy of my invention. I had successfully defended my PhD, which was my life's dream, and was slated for graduation.

But then I was confronted with another question: What in the world should I do after graduation?

I never wanted to become a professor, which was a typical career path for PhDs from MIT. I had no desire to teach, to grade papers, to oversee students. I had benefited greatly from educators, of course, but I wanted to do something different with my life, something that would continue to help people who had suffered tremendous loss.

Money was never the aim. Both Laurie and I had been brought up to be content with what we had, to make do. During my PhD work, we'd been comfortable financially. But after graduation, as I looked at the biomedical landscape unfolding before me, I knew that money had to be in my future. If I wanted to make a significant contribution, I'd need significant resources.

I'd often heard it said, "Where there is no vision, the people perish" (Proverbs 29:18). But without money, I came to realize, the vision perishes. I needed a grant, a company to underwrite the cost of my vision. And when I learned that MIT would be patenting my invention, I was overjoyed.

Bringing my idea to fruition, though, and seeing it embraced by surgical oncologists, was an entirely different challenge. As it turned out, surgeons at that time viewed restoring the voice as far too risky an endeavor, one requiring a demanding and time-consuming surgery that wasn't necessary for their primary goal of saving the patient's life. Instead, they preferred to focus on the delicate art of resecting tumors without the added difficulties of inserting a pathway for an artificial vocal cord. Without surgeons on board to champion my product, I hit a brick wall. I soon realized that, like so many other promising technologies before it, nothing more would ever come of my prototype or patent.

Without a promising prospect for this technology, I needed to find a job focusing on something else. Professor Shapiro put me in touch with an MIT alum who was working on a start-up company doing blood separation. "It involves a lot of fluid mechanics, Don," he said. "Stuff you know really well."

The possibility of working in the burgeoning field of blood separation fascinated me, so I interviewed for the job and began with a starting salary of $19,000 a year—a modest paycheck for a PhD from MIT. But with the job came a stock option, and I knew that would be key. With the right discovery, and with a financial stake in the company, I'd be positioned to do something significant in this world.

All of my education was about to pay off.

11

BLOOD AND SWEAT

Irvine, California
April 1981

After I graduated from MIT, my professional life blossomed, and within a few years, so did our family. Our first daughter arrived in 1981, and with the birth of our second, Laurie decided to quit her job and stay home. By the time our third arrived, Laurie had her hands full with spunky, spirited girls.

Laurie dedicated her life to filling her home with tender love. She sought to bless others first and was always ready to help and support anyone who needed it, especially our daughters. She taxied the girls and their friends to endless volleyball matches and Girl Scout troop meetings. She drove our family on cross-country vacations, eventually wearing out not one but *two* fifteen-passenger vans. She taught our family how to appreciate history, literature, culture, and kindness, and she even taught this engineer how to love.

I had my hands full as well. Over the next decade and a half, from my graduation from MIT until the mid-1990s, my career led me into the new and burgeoning field of blood cell separation. It was in this field that I first hoped to leave a legacy. For several years, I worked with startup companies on blood separation before an interesting conversation one day with a man named Bill Miller. He was an entrepreneur, and his ideas resonated with me.

"Don," he said, "let's come up with something that we could turn into a product." Bill would be the business manager, I would be the science and engineering guy, and together we would develop a new technology that would shake up the field of medical diagnostics and make us a lot of money in the process.

Since the 1960s, researchers had explored ways to glean medical information from analyzing the liquid sweat coming from the pores in the skin. They failed because they did not have a reliable method of collecting sweat in its liquid form. The concept was abandoned.

Meanwhile, wound care technology was changing dramatically. In the past, people would get allergic reactions to the white tape used for bandages. It was discovered that these reactions were caused by the water content of sweat. In the 1980s researchers developed a bandage composed of a very thin layer of polyurethane, just thin enough to allow water vapor molecules to pass to the air, but not allowing larger molecules to escape or allowing bacteria and the like to enter the wound site. The company 3M acquired this technology and introduced a new line of wound care products called Tegaderm. Tegaderm completely revolutionized wound dressing. Tegaderm avoided the allergic reactions because liquid sweat evaporated as water vapor through the thin polyurethane layer.

Surgeons also found a great use for Tegaderm. They'd wrap a wide roll of it on their patients before an operation to prevent skin bacteria from invading an open surgical site. The tape could stay on the skin for an entire month.

Don Schoendorfer

But what would happen, I wondered, if I were to look at what is retained under a Tegaderm bandage after a few hours, a week, or a month? Would the residue have a diagnostic value? What if I could develop a patch that would harvest what came through the skin, excluding the evaporated water content? All I needed to do is place a piece of gauze under a layer of Tegaderm on the skin, leave it on for say a week, remove the gauze, send it to the lab, and measure its residue in all sorts of ways.

I didn't have a proper lab to do the work. But plenty of other inventions, at one time or another, have had their origins in someone's garage, so I converted part of my garage into a research facility where I could measure sweat and see what it contained.

I discovered that, indeed, all sorts of significant diagnostic information was contained in the residue. Everything started to point toward success. My discoveries were groundbreaking. I gathered a scientific advisory committee that helped us understand diagnostic chemistry.

"We need to get this idea through the FDA," I told Bill. The goal was how to make this idea into a product that had a real-world, industry-changing application.

After five very long years of testing on me, on my family, on Bill's family, and then through formal clinical trials, we finally succeeded. The FDA cleared the concept to use as a method to collect transdermal analytes for diagnostic applications.

The patch we developed was soon showing unlimited potential. We realized that our invention could be used to measure everything from drug abuse, early markers of osteoporosis, tissue damage from reduced blood flow to the heart, or chemical markers from silent ischemia.

We had a plan to reach the masses with our technology. Imagine this. You're flipping through a magazine—say, *Woman's Day* or *Redbook*—and you see our advertisement with the patch affixed to the page. You read the instructions: Tear off the patch, place it on your skin, wear it for a week, mail it to our lab, and for ten dollars the lab could tell you if you should see your doctor to find out if you were likely to suffer from life-threatening diseases in the future. It was a wellness patch.

Simple as that. No needles required for blood samples, no vials for urine samples. Just a small patch that cost less than a dollar to manufacture and could be mailed to a lab in a regular envelope.

We realized that we were possibly sitting on a technology with huge potential—a gold mine, a real treasure. We were going to change the medical diagnostics industry forever.

3M gave us seed money. They manufactured the patch for us. As soon as we found a company to buy our technology, we would be billionaires. We could feel it.

Sure, the costs and risks were high. We'd invested a lot of money in securing patents, and we'd spent tens of thousands of dollars to set up a solid business structure so that when we sold the technology, our profits would be managed well. But we were confident—no, more than that, we were *certain*—that the returns would far surpass the expenditures.

We knew we needed very strong patents to secure funding. We built a family of patents on the patch, on its application and methods of analysis. There was no way anyone else could work around these patents to produce a product similar to ours, a product that was even remotely close to being practical.

We were in a lane of our own, chomping at the bit, waiting for the gun.

Little did we know just how much blood and sweat the race would eventually cost us.

12

SURRENDER

Santa Ana, California
May 1994

Mathematically speaking, there are only ten digits—zero to nine. It sounds simple: put these numbers into any specific formula, and the result is predictable and infinite. Laurie and I had a shared plan for how we would raise our children. We sought out the best schools and extracurricular activities. Laurie dedicated her time to being a stay-at-home mom so that our daughters wouldn't miss any opportunities available to them. We were confident that they would thrive having the life we had for ourselves, and that all would be well.

When one of our daughters reached eighth grade, the plan failed. It was the beginning of a long, difficult journey—the first of many times that we'd have to turn to experts for help with our girls.

We discovered that she had an eating disorder and had been battling it secretly for several months. First, we took her to see a psychiatrist who prescribed medication that didn't seem to help.

Then, we found a psychologist who thought she could deal with eating disorders, but this, too, got us nowhere.

I put my research skills to work trying to figure out a way to solve this terrible problem that was tormenting our daughter. I interviewed the world's experts on eating disorders and pored over academic articles, long after everyone else had gone to sleep. I discovered that the experts fell into two camps—one that said you can't do anything about it, that you just have to keep them alive and let it run its course, and the other that said that if you don't do something about it, it'll get worse. I was stuck in the middle, hoping it would go away.

A year passed. We didn't know how to help our little girl, and she was getting worse and worse. I felt utterly helpless, watching as she was consumed by self-loathing and sadness, and I had no formula for solving the problem.

Finally, she came to Laurie and me in desperation: "I need help. I can't do this on my own."

I knew we had money in the bank, and I was willing to spend every cent of it to help our daughter get well. We began researching inpatient facilities, knowing we'd send her to the very best treatment facility money could buy.

We eventually found a place with promise, a ranch with horses and therapy and treatment. The founder of the organization had become a Christian in the course of helping his own daughter be cured of bulimia. We arrived not knowing what to expect, and before we could even talk logistics, they prayed with us. Laurie and I both thought it was a bit odd, but they had the best reputation of any treatment facility we'd investigated, so we decided to stick with it. We left before we could change our mind.

We returned home and told our daughter the plan. A few days later, we three traveled to Arizona, only five hours by car, but too far away for our comfort. Our intention was to drop her off for a ninety-day residential treatment program. The cost was $30,000 a month. As we checked her in at the front desk, I looked around. Some of the residents looked like they were on their deathbeds: skin and bones, and not much more.

We said our goodbyes, and it took all the strength we had to leave. We knew that the only way to help our daughter was to surrender her to these professionals. I slipped my arm around Laurie's shoulder, and we turned toward the door.

Moments later, just as we stepped outside, I heard cries of desperation, and I turned around to see her running toward the door, sobbing. "Please don't leave me here!" she cried, tears streaming down her flushed cheeks. We'd been told to expect this, but it sure didn't make things any easier. I squeezed Laurie's hand, and we continued through the exit.

Only one thought filled my mind as Laurie and I made our way to the car:

Please, let this work.

———————

After several weeks, Laurie and I received word that we would be allowed to visit our daughter. We had no idea what to expect but loaded up the car and began the five-hour drive east.

We arrived a bit early and had the option of either waiting in the car or sitting in on the service in the chapel. Out in the desert, the temperature had risen to well over a hundred degrees. We chose the chapel. As it turned out, we were just in time for the service.

We sat near the back of the chapel, and soon our daughter joined us. Laurie and I each gave her a long hug, relieved to have her in our arms once again and desperate to learn how she was faring.

Twenty or so of our daughter's peers sat near the front of the small chapel, teenagers also battling eating disorders, some with IV stands for the intravenous feeding that was keeping them alive. Half a dozen parents sat near us in the back. A man stood at the front and began to read from the Bible.

I didn't pay very close attention until I heard him offer a challenge to his tiny congregation.

"I want you to come up with a definition of love," he said. He waited a few seconds and then began on one side of the room, asking each of the young women to offer their answers. I quickly realized that I was going to be the first adult he got to after making his way through the adolescent patients, and I knew he'd expect me to have an intelligent answer. Everyone would, but I couldn't think of anything meaningful to say. Not a single thing. Laurie and I didn't really talk openly about things like this, and besides, I'm an engineer . . . what did I know about love?

What on earth am I going to say? I could feel drops of perspiration forming on my brow. *What's going to make sense?* I was sweating bullets.

I'm going to let my daughter down.

The last patient offered her definition, and to my great surprise, instead of turning to me, the preacher opened his Bible and began to read from 1 Corinthians 13. "Love is patient, love is kind . . ."

I exhaled slowly and tried to stifle my relieved chuckle. I'd been saved by the Bible! I wiped the beads of sweat from my forehead and listened as the preacher continued on about love. "It does not envy, it does not boast, it is not proud. It does not dishonor others, it is not self-seeking, it is not easily angered, it keeps no record of wrongs. Love does not delight in evil but rejoices with the truth. It always protects, always trusts, always hopes, always perseveres" (NIV).

I grew up going to Sunday school and church every week,

daydreaming about my boat while at church, but religion had never really "stuck." I still couldn't see a place for God in my life. Ever since college, I'd been questioning religion, and I hadn't gotten very far. Neither Laurie nor I had been practicing any sort of faith very visibly for some time now, but these words from the Bible seemed to make sense. I didn't think I could have come up with a better definition of love.

This is insightful stuff, I thought. *Whoever wrote this really thought it through.* I opened the Bible in front of me and started to flip through it. I'd always viewed the Bible as a valuable piece of literature, and I knew there were good things in there, but I didn't think they'd apply to anything I had to deal with.

I chewed on the question during our drive back home, and for several weeks after. Before long, we received another call from the treatment facility. "Your daughter is doing much better," her therapist said. "If you'd like, you can come out again for another visit."

We left California early on Sunday and arrived in late morning, just in time to take her to the only approved destination outside of her treatment facility: church. The woman staffing the facility lobby handed us a list of options, and we picked one arbitrarily from her list.

The three of us piled into the family car and drove to nearby Phoenix. I was surprised to see that the church was meeting in a high school gymnasium. We had arrived late, so we snuck quietly into the back with our daughter nestled between Laurie and me. The pastor was speaking.

He was talking about problems—his own problems, his problems with his wife and kids, his problems with his faith. In all the years, decades even, that I'd gone to church back home in Ashtabula, I'd never once heard the pastor mention his own problems. Whenever he talked about difficulties, they were always someone else's. I grew up thinking the pastor had never had a problem in his entire life. And if he didn't have any of his own, then I shouldn't be talking to him about any of mine.

At the end of the service, our daughter grabbed my hand. I looked down and realized that she'd grabbed Laurie's hand as well, and soon, she was dragging us down to the front of the gymnasium. I looked up the raised platform at the pastor, then glanced over to Laurie. Neither of us knew what to say. Suddenly, our daughter blurted out, "These are my parents, and they have to start going to church!"

I didn't exactly know what to say to the pastor, nor did Laurie, but I had to offer something, so I said something about my experiences growing up in church in the '60s. "I really admire you for being so vulnerable in your sermon," I said. "I'm wondering if there are any churches like this one in Orange County. One that would have a similar presentation?"

The man thought for a second. "Mariners Church," he said. "I'm told it's pretty similar to what we do here."

The idea of going to a weekly worship service wasn't something I could envision fitting into my life, and I wasn't about to commit to anything, but I nodded and thanked him for the advice. "Well," I said, "maybe we'll go there."

The very next week, I found myself sitting in a pew at Mariners Church.

13

THE FOOL'S GAME

Irvine, California
November 1996

O ver that first year attending Mariners Church, I went from being a "pedestrian Christian"—someone merely standing on the sidewalk and watching other people practice their faith—to wanting much more. For the first time in my life, I felt God working on me, slowly opening my eyes to what had been there all along. I felt a need to get out on the street myself and start *doing* something, instead of just passively attending church on Sunday.

I tried volunteering at our church's Learning Center, teaching math and science to immigrants from Central America. With my background, I figured that would be a good fit, but boy, was I wrong. I knew math and science well enough, but I had no idea how to teach them to adolescents. Then I learned about the church's mentor program. *Maybe I'd be better off helping people with their lives, not their schoolwork,* I thought.

The first young man I mentored was out on parole and sleeping in cars. It was my first real attempt at personally connecting with someone who was significantly less privileged than me. When he went back to jail, though, our mentorship fizzled.

The next person I was assigned to mentor was younger, which was hard because no matter what I tried, I just couldn't connect. Before long, I knew that I wasn't going to be very successful with him either. *I'm just not good enough to be a mentor.*

From there, I went on tutoring other students, but I wasn't making any real difference, at least not a discernible one. At that low point, it felt like God began to talk to me. He'd probably been speaking to me all along, but now I started to listen.

Don! God seemed to say. *I want to talk about how you're spending your time.*

Okay . . .

I know you're an introvert, God said. *You don't like people in general, I've really noticed that. You barely got through your psychology class in college. You're not trained as an educator. You have no knowledge about being a mentor. And quite frankly, I'm discouraged that you're not using the tools that I gave you.*

What tools would those be, Lord? I wondered.

You're an engineer, aren't you? As an engineer, can't you come up with something that would help my kingdom?

———————

One day, in a Sunday-morning church service, pastor Kenton Beshore said something that changed my life. He shared a story that couldn't have been more than four sentences long, and he called it "The Fool's Game."

As the story goes, the fool is a person who wants to do something good—for the world, for God, for society, for whatever—but he's got

Don Schoendorfer

this long list of things that he has to get done first. He also has another list, one full of things he really wants to do someday, and that list is getting longer, too. As soon as something gets checked off the first list, another thing gets added, and the list never gets any shorter. There's always one more thing to do, one more thing to cross off, and then he dies. He spent his entire life playing The Fool's Game, and he lost.

It's a huge church— about three thousand people in the sanctuary at the time—yet I swore that the pastor was talking directly to me.

This is exactly what I've been doing, I realized.

I wanted to become comfortable financially. I wanted to get my kids through college, the best colleges possible, Ivy League schools on the East Coast. I wanted to help my daughter get rid of her eating disorder and keep her alive with treatment programs, no matter how expensive they were. I had all these things to worry about, one after the next. But I wasn't accomplishing anything significant.

That's when I took an honest assessment of my life. I had a lot of patents. I'd made some companies wealthy at the expense of other companies. Maybe I'd helped a few people in hospitals speed up the healing process, but that didn't strike me as terribly significant compared to what I *could* be doing.

I'm the fool, I concluded. *Something's got to change.*

———————

For years while we lived in Boston, Laurie had enjoyed collecting antiques. She adored spending the day scavenging through open-air markets and yard sales, hunting for eclectic things to stash in our living room. She especially loved visiting the enormous parks on the weekends where everybody came to sell their wares. It was rather boring, but I tagged along to support her.

One day, long before moving to California and before our children were born, we'd been walking through a field surrounded by relics and all kinds of junk from the past when my eyes came to rest on an antique wheelchair. It was oak and wicker, and it was a mess.

But there was something about that chair that mesmerized me, fascinated me. I felt drawn to it, almost like it was pulling me in its direction. The seller wasn't asking much for it, so I pulled out my wallet, handed him all of twenty-five bucks, and rolled the wheelchair back to the van.

Over that Christmas, I gave myself entirely to refurbishing the chair. I restitched its cane, stripped its wood, and gave it a fresh glaze of polyurethane.

"Why do you insist on keeping this wheelchair in the living room?" Laurie asked me one day.

I didn't know, exactly. "It kind of goes with the antiques," I said. I didn't know just *how* antique it was until, a little while later, I was reading a book about the Civil War and saw a black-and-white photo of a wheelchair that looked just like mine. It had the same design, the same construction, the same wicker, everything.

"This thing's from the Civil War era!" I said to Laurie, hoping it would change her perspective. Laurie was right. The chair really was an eyesore, to use her word. Yet every day I'd walk past it and wonder how many wounded soldiers that chair had served, how many people over the centuries had put their weight on it.

One afternoon, as I walked through our living room past the eyesore of a wheelchair, I suddenly stopped dead in my tracks. My thoughts snapped back to Morocco, to that woman in the marketplace, with her bloodied hands and blistered feet. I remembered how people tried to avoid stepping on her, how they jumped out of her way as she dragged her body across the cobblestones.

How many people are there just like her in the world? I wondered. *How many people could be lifted up off the ground if they only had a wheelchair?*

I began to do some research on wheelchairs in the United States. Most of them looked like they belonged in a hospital, not a home. *I wonder if there's a way to make a wheelchair look more like a living room chair, only with wheels,* I thought. I took out my journal, dated April 1999. It contained a few experimental pencil sketches that I'd made of the medical products I was working on—an old habit I picked up during my doctoral work when I needed to get my thoughts down on paper.

I didn't know much about how to build a wheelchair. By definition, I knew that I needed two wheels and a chair, at the very minimum. I knew that oak, like my Civil War–era chair, would be too expensive to manufacture in bulk, so I began sketching out designs for a prototype that would be durable yet lightweight, easy to produce, and affordable to transport. Several materials crossed my mind: steel, metal, plastic. But for the longest time, I was stuck.

I kept asking myself, *What's the least expensive, most durable chair in the world?*

We were approaching the end of lawn-furniture season in California when the answer suddenly came out of the blue.

The white resin lawn chair.

They were all around me, these chairs—scattered across backyards, patios, and pools. They were easy to clean and remarkably inexpensive to buy, especially in the fall. Because they're white, they'd be cool in the summer, and they're actually quite comfortable to sit in.

Having worked in the medical disposable industry, I'd seen the strength of these chairs made from polyethylene resin. It's an inexpensive, disposable, lightweight material often used for processing components of expensive electronic equipment. White resin is a common material, not unique, which meant that it could be manufactured in large quantities.

The challenge before me was intriguing. I'd figure out a way for a white resin lawn chair to work as a wheelchair. It would be an enjoyable mental exercise, the task of proving it could be done, and I was excited at the prospect of designing a prototype. *And who knows,* I thought, *maybe one day someone might even decide to manufacture this wheelchair.*

———————

In the months that followed, I tinkered with the design. I found that it had become a passion project of sorts, something to keep me busy in my spare time.

Having settled on the white resin, I next turned my attention to the wheels. I picked up the phone and called a few wheelchair manufacturers.

"Hey," I'd say, "I have an idea, and I'd like to buy some wheelchair wheels from you."

"Hold on, sir," the voice on the other end would say. "What do you plan to do with these wheelchairs?"

"I'm not exactly sure. But I think I'm going to give them away in developing countries."

There was always a pause, and then, "Well, give me your number, and we'll call you back."

They never did. I was getting nowhere and didn't know why. There had to be another way.

In every country that Laurie and I had visited, we'd seen people riding bicycles. According to an article in *Scientific American,* which I had read years earlier, bicycles were the world's most common form of transportation, not cars. I began to consider incorporating bicycle wheels into my designs. They would be perfect for rugged terrain.

Surely there must be hundreds of companies that could produce bicycle wheels, I reasoned. *Like, in the gazillions.*

Somewhere in the year 2000, amid all the little wheelchair vignettes that I'd sketched in my journal, I wrote the following entry: "Company contact info for bicycle wheels." Beneath it were email addresses I'd collected from the internet, which had only recently experienced widespread usage.

It was tough going, especially because most bicycle wheel companies didn't yet have websites. The ones who did were located in countries like China, and they didn't always have a representative who responded to my emails in English.

When I began searching for companies that gave away wheelchairs to people in developing countries, the results were meager. Netscape, the search engine at the time, only produced a few hits—fifteen to twenty, tops—and most of those were volunteer groups.

If I was going to focus on helping people who lived in developing countries, I had to admit that I didn't know much about those places. When Laurie and I traveled, we traveled as tourists, visiting wealthy areas, staying in nice hotels. The extent of my knowledge of developing countries came almost exclusively from reading *National Geographic.* I'd often flip through the photos, shocked at what I saw, trying to put myself in their shoes, in their feet, imagining how life must feel.

After what seemed like an eternity of phone calls, I finally located a company in China with a representative, whom I affectionately nicknamed my "Wheelman," with whom I could communicate in English via email. I explained my situation, and he agreed to sell me twenty-four-inch wheels for my prototype. I was overjoyed, and the second they arrived, I dashed to my garage to assemble the chair.

Of course, I didn't have all the right tools I needed to make a top-notch, first-rate wheelchair. Instead of using strong steel tubing for a frame, which I didn't have the equipment to bend, I chose instead to use conduit, a thin-walled tubing about three fourths of an inch in diameter. It was not nearly as sturdy as true steel tubing, but it was bendable.

I shaped the silver-colored conduit into an arc for the frame, attached the wheels, put the lawn chair in it, and then added the two small casters in the front for stability. Finally, I stepped back to look at my creation.

It was rudimentary, no doubt. Basic. There was no footrest, just a chair with four wheels. But as I lowered my weight onto the seat, I knew that my prototype would work. When I pushed the wheels with my arms and hands, the chair rolled forward, then backward, then in circles.

Sitting there in my garage, in my mobile lawn chair, after so many months of conceptualizing its design, and contacting companies, and securing manufacturers, and assembling my prototype, I felt that I had finally done something significant. I'd created something that might just help people in need.

In that moment, as I sat in my wheelchair in the garage, not far from the Civil War wheelchair in the living room, I thought back to the hard question God had put before me: *Don, what have you done for my kingdom?*

I was sitting in the answer.

Don with his parents and older brothers George
(second from right) and Carl (right).

An eleven-year-old Don tinkers with a slide rule in his
brother's dorm room.

Don, taking *Sailfish* out on Canada's Lake Nipissing.

Twelve-year-old Don test drives his go-kart prototype.

The Schoendorters at Don's graduation from Columbia in 1972.

Don, newly arrived in Boston and ready for MIT, 1972.

Don and Laurie while on vacation in Morocco.

Don and Laurie's wedding day, 1974.

Just married: the best man drives Don and Laurie in *ZigZag*, the van named after its loose steering system.

Testing artificial vocal cords at an MIT lab in
1975 with Dr. Steve Raymond (right).

In the Santa Ana, California, garage where Don began to
develop a line of cost-efficient, durable wheelchairs.

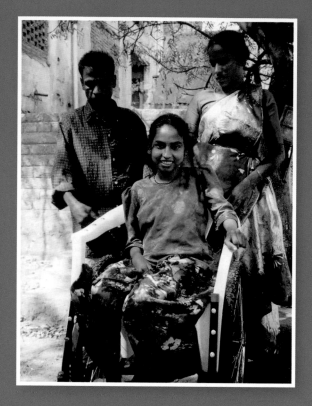

Lotus Blossom, one week after receiving her first wheelchair in 2001.

Indra, a young woman in Chennai, India, received one of the first four of Don's wheelchairs in 2001.

Angola, 2001, when Don set out to distribute forty-three of the first one hundred wheelchairs he had made in his garage.

The iconic-but-now-retired GEN_1 model wheelchairs developed by Don.

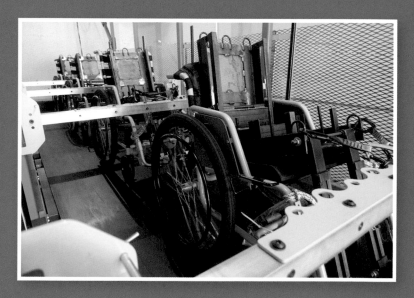

Lotus, the innovative wheelchair test track at Free Wheelchair Mission headquarters in Irvine, California.

Some of the many ways to deliver wheelchairs to those in need in remote regions.

To Don Schoendorfer
With best wishes,

Receiving the White House Call to Service Award in 2007, with President George W. Bush.

Receiving the Above and Beyond Citizen Award in 2008, with General Colin Powell.

Rollout of the GEN_2 model in Zambia, 2012.

Laurie on a trip to Peru in 2003, distributing wheelchairs to a sister and a brother who had not seen one another in years.

Don, Laurie, and their three daughters in 2010.

With Francis Mugwanya, founder of Father's Heart Mobility Ministry in Uganda, a longtime Free Wheelchair Mission distribution partner.

Transforming a
life in Vietnam.

Assembling a GEN_2 wheelchair in Guatemala, 2019.

Misole (seated), a schoolteacher who had lost mobility to injuries sustained in the 2010 Haiti earthquake.

A team from Camino de Vida Church prays with a wheelchair recipient in Peru.

Linh, who started a small business after receiving her wheelchair, sewed masks for the community in the early months of the COVID-19 pandemic.

The GEN_3 wheelchair folds for ease of storage and transport in urban settings.

The foldable GEN_3 can easily squeeze through narrow doorways and into tight quarters.

The smiles and joy of those who finally receive the wheelchair they have been waiting for are priceless.

One wheelchair can make a life-changing impact on an entire family and their community.

Laurie on her last wheelchair distribution trip in the fall of 2015.

The joy that comes from receiving a new wheelchair is contagious.

Peru, 2017. With Flor (seated), the recipient of Free Wheelchair Mission's one-millionth wheelchair.

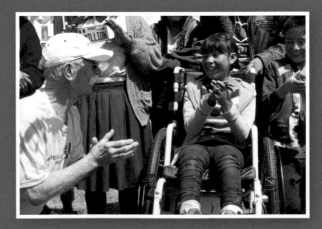

14

IT'S OVER

Santa Ana, California
March 1999

O ver the years, I worked on blood cell separation (apheresis) and the development of medical diagnostic technologies with a variety of exciting start-up companies—Haemonetics, HemaScience Laboratories, Baxter Travenol, Fenwal, and finally Sudormed.

One afternoon in the spring of 1999, as I sat at my desk at Sudormed working on developing a new kind of patch that would have the capability to test for alcohol in the body, my partner burst into the lab.

"The rep from 3M is flying in from St. Paul tomorrow," he said. "This is it, Don!"

The timing couldn't have been better. We'd been having some trouble generating big interest from the diagnostic companies, and 3M knew it. We needed an extra boost, hopefully another million, or at least several hundred thousand, and headquarters was sending their representative to tell us the good news in person.

Just before lunchtime, the representative arrived at our office. I'd dressed for the occasion, too, wearing a decent dress shirt for a change.

"Gentlemen," he said, "I'm afraid I have some bad news."

I shot a quick glance at my partner. *Bad news?*

"I'm coming with my hat in my hands, guys, because unfortunately I've been sent to tell you that it's over."

"Over?" my partner, Bill, asked. "What do you mean, it's over?"

"We've already given you quite a bit of money, and there's not much to show for it at this point. The company's concerned that we won't be able to get anyone to buy your technology." He paused, then shifted awkwardly in his seat, eyes down. "And I'm afraid there's more bad news."

More bad news?

"We would love to get our money back from you, but we know you're a start-up, and that you had to tread water for five years until the FDA accepted your work."

His words didn't immediately register. The barb was set, but it took a few seconds for the poison to sink in.

The rep continued. "So the only option we have is to accept your patents in place of the funds."

"The patents?" my partner said, equally shaken. "How many of them?"

"All of them."

In that moment, and with those three words, I realized the implications of his statement. It was over. Without the patents, there'd be no way for us to continue development of the alcohol patch. The technology we created would no longer belong to us. We'd have nothing to sell.

We had no choice. We couldn't pay back the money.

I let out a slow, painful sigh, and with it went a decade's worth of work. Not only were my dreams suddenly dashed to pieces, but all the trappings would disappear as well. The paycheck, the office, the furniture . . . even the chair I was sitting in. We'd have to sell that, too.

But something else disappeared in that meeting. Something that caused a deeper pain.

Ever since my days at MIT, ever since I first saw the opportunities Uncle George's wealth had afforded him, I had wanted to become a billionaire. I wanted to do new things to help people and without all the hassles of asking others for financial help. But in that moment, even that desire to have the kind of money that would allow me to do something significant in this world vanished as well.

It was over.

15

PROTOTYPE

Santa Ana, California
April 1999

O ne of the things I learned from working in the engineering industry is that having a dream is not enough. If you want to sell your dream, you've got to build a prototype for people to see, touch, and test for themselves.

Laurie eyed my newly assembled prototype in the garage. "So, what are you going to do next?" she asked.

"I don't know," I said. "But I might know someone who does."

I picked up the phone and made an appointment with Skip Lanfried, the outreach pastor at Mariners Church. Hopefully, he would have an idea about what my next step should be.

It was a Thursday afternoon, one never to be forgotten. I pulled into the crowded church parking lot and circled it a few times before squeezing into an empty space. *What's going on?* I wondered. *It's a Thursday—why are all these cars here?* I marveled at how Mariners could pack a church, not just on a Sunday, but on a weekday.

There was a flurry of activity inside the building, people

everywhere. I walked to the Outreach department. Skip was waiting to greet me at the door and take me back into his office.

"I've got this crazy idea," I said, getting right down to business.

"Okay, let's hear it."

"I think the world needs wheelchairs."

Skip looked at me curiously, not saying a word. He'd just returned from an international mission trip, and I could see the jet lag in his eyes.

"I don't know how many people in the world actually need wheelchairs," I said. "And nobody else does either. The World Health Organization has determined that there are 75 million, but that's just an estimation. Do you really think it could be that bad?"

Skip nodded. "I can't tell you about the numbers," he said, "but I *can* tell you about how I saw people crawling on the ground just two days ago in the Democratic Republic of the Congo. They weren't crawling for show, either. These people just needed to get from one place to another."

I took a deep breath and dove right in. "I've got this prototype, Skip," I said.

"A prototype?"

"Yes, a prototype of a wheelchair. Built it in my garage."

Skip's eyes lit up.

"It's in my car," I continued, "but I don't want you to get too excited about it, cause it's just a prototype. It's not really ready to roll around too much."

"Well, what are we waiting for?" Skip exclaimed, springing out of his jet lag. "Let's go try it out!"

I felt a small panic in the pit of my stomach. When I arranged this meeting, I'd only intended to *tell* Skip about the prototype. It hadn't occurred to me that he'd actually want to test it out.

"Okay," I acquiesced. "But like I said, don't get too excited about it."

Before I knew it, we were leaving the building, making our way through the parking lot and to the van, which I unlocked. Skip helped me remove the wheelchair, and not a second later he had blasted off in the thing, rolling around the asphalt, taking twists and hard turns, having the time of his life.

I held my breath, waiting for the crash, certain that the wheels would fly off, and I'd witness my outreach pastor, whom I'd just met, wipe out on the concrete and injure himself.

Skip had an audience, too. As he was rolling around the parking lot, mulling over the possibilities of the wheelchair, I noticed that a couple of ladies were watching him as well. As it turned out, they'd also just returned from an international mission trip.

I was standing close enough to the action to overhear one woman say to the other, "Don't you think that would be a good wheelchair for people in developing countries?" I was startled. The other woman nodded as they continued to watch Skip maneuver the wheelchair beside the curb.

Everything in me was saying *yes*.

Yes, this *would* be a good wheelchair for people in developing countries. It could change their lives. These women were thinking the same thing I was thinking, the same thing Skip was now thinking.

This can't be a coincidence, I thought. *This has to be providence.*

I managed to tear Skip out of the chair, and we returned to his office to hash out the details.

"We've got to get a handle on this," he said.

I felt the same way. But I knew that to make this happen, to prove that it would be possible for someone to manufacture durable, inexpensive wheelchairs and give them away in the developing world, would be no small undertaking. And I couldn't do it alone. I needed guidance and direction from people who did this sort of thing full time, not part time. There were answers I didn't have to questions I didn't even know to ask.

"Where do we start?" I asked.

Skip thought for a second. "Okay, first, what are you going to do for supply?"

I shrugged my shoulders. Didn't have a clue.

"You'd better look into that first," Skip said. "I'll help as much as I can."

We discussed a few additional key steps I needed to take. I left his office and walked back to my car, a newfound mission in tow. Pulling out of the parking lot, I shot a glance in the rearview mirror. The wheelchair hadn't fallen apart, as I'd feared. Quite the opposite, in fact. The prototype held up brilliantly.

I couldn't wait to get home to tell Laurie all about it. She'd be so thrilled to learn that all the tinkering I'd been doing in the garage for all these years wasn't just a hobby that occupied my time. The energy had been worth the effort. And the wheelchair, which I couldn't stop glancing at, was turning into something bigger than the both of us.

———

There was a humanitarian group that met near the Boeing facility in north Los Angeles called Wheels for Humanity. I'd come across them in my quest to figure out how to transport wheelchairs to other countries. Most of the volunteers were retired engineers, machinists, and mechanics brought together by a common cause: to refurbish worn-out wheelchairs that had been donated to them by individuals and families whose medical insurance had replaced their old wheelchairs with brand-new ones—and then give them away.

"Where do you send your wheelchairs?" I asked them.

"To South America."

"And how do you transport them?"

"We ship them in huge containers."

That made sense as an affordable way to get the chairs to other countries. "And how do you give them away after they arrive?" I asked.

"Well, we have people down there who help us do the final assembly. There's a lot of adjustments that need to be made to the chairs for each person."

"What if something breaks?" I asked. "How do you fix it?"

There was just silence. No answer. They knew that their wheelchairs would be difficult to fix, because they were all different models with unique parts and accessories. I had to avoid this problem, because one look at the size of their warehouse of parts made me realize how important it is to keep the design simple.

But who could produce all the parts that I needed for my prototype? I thought about the first question Skip had asked me. *What am I going to do for supply?*

I tracked down a source of wheels in China. So I called my friend Wheelman and asked if he was willing to sell me two hundred wheels and two hundred casters. All I had to do was pick up the crate at the port of Los Angeles. "You better get there early," he said. "Things get very busy there, and you will be surrounded by containers and container-hauling trucks."

That turned out to be a real experience.

When the notice arrived, informing me that my shipment was ready to be retrieved, I didn't have a vehicle large enough to get them back to my house, so I rented a U-Haul trailer and drove to San Pedro Bay, about twenty-five miles south of the downtown area, to the port of Los Angeles—the busiest port in the entire Western Hemisphere, a massive complex covering some forty-three miles of waterfront.

By the time I arrived at the port, around 5:00 a.m., there was already a mile of semitrailers lined up bumper to bumper, a long chain of red brake lights, all of them ready to pick up their loads. I waited several hours in that line, inching my way closer before finally pulling my van and trailer into Pier E.

There was a lot where all the container rigs were located, and I decided that was where I needed to go. I parked the van and walked into the building, only to find myself waiting in another line, a long line of drivers. I listened to the conversations buzzing around me in Cambodian, Vietnamese, and Spanish. Nobody spoke English. I'd never done this before, which quickly became obvious to everyone, and especially to the clerk working the counter.

"Here's my paperwork," I said, handing my documents to the woman. "How do I proceed to get my cargo?"

I was instructed to back the trailer up to the loading dock so I could handle the shipment. The thing was, I've never been good at backing up a trailer. So there I was, pulling forward and backward, trying to get the end of the trailer lined up with the loading dock. I would go six inches ahead, then six inches in reverse. *Nope.* Then a foot forward, then two feet backward. *Nope.*

This happened over and over, going forward and then backward. It was a humiliating experience, and as the minutes passed, I could see that my clumsy maneuvering had attracted an audience of about thirty truck drivers who were laughing their heads off at me. Eventually, the amusement wore off, and out of great pity, or heroism, or annoyance, one of the truck drivers came over and tapped on my window.

"Let me do it," he said.

The weight of the crate tested the horsepower of my van as I drove back home—a journey that moved the needle of my speedometer not a single hair over thirty-five miles per hour. When I arrived, I parked the trailer on the street, opened the back of the trailer, and unloaded the cargo into my garage.

With my garage crammed full of two hundred bicycle wheels and two hundred casters, I knew it was time to progress to the next phase of the wheelchair's development: finding a company to manufacture the frame, preferably a local company.

The next day, I visited several fabricators in Los Angeles. I showed them some of the drawings I'd made and the conduit model that I'd bent into various arcs. But as I was talking to them, I began to notice a pattern in all their responses.

"How many frames do you want?" they'd ask.

"A hundred."

"Only a hundred? Sorry, we can't help you."

Nobody wanted to produce such a small quantity of frames. It just wasn't cost-effective for them. Perhaps if I'd needed a few thousand frames instead of a mere hundred, I might have been more successful. But every manufacturer I approached turned me down.

Finally, I found a Christian company that looked promising. As I pulled into the parking lot, I noticed a huge fish on the outside of the building. *That's got to be a good sign*, I reasoned.

It was an ancient symbol, the fish. I'd learned in church that in the first-century Mediterranean world, when Christianity was illegal, believers would draw the sign of the fish as a sort of secret code that brought like-minded people together. That fish also reminded me of my dad, and that time we spent fishing on Lake Erie, and all those fish fries that my brothers and I attended.

At the time, I hated getting to the front of the line, starving and drooling at the smell of freshly fried fish while my dad insisted on letting everyone else cut in front of us. But now, as I parked my car and walked inside the building, I knew I needed someone willing to put my interests above their own.

"I'm getting desperate, guys," I told them. "I've been up here for days trying to find a fabricator. All I want to do is make a hundred frames for wheelchairs to give away to people in developing countries." I couldn't believe the response.

"We can make them for you," they said.

"You can make only a hundred of them?" I wasn't sure I'd heard them correctly.

"Sure," they said. "It'll cost you twenty-five dollars per frame."

It was an answer to prayer, an answer to the problem of supply that I'd grown weary of solving. We shook on it, and I drove home, grateful and ready to tackle the last remaining obstacle in my way: how to store all these wheelchairs.

In California, most people park their cars outside on the driveway, but even in our three-car garage, which we used as a storage area, workshop, and machine lab, the space was tight.

After all the components arrived, I spent a few weeks assembling them. I had to make sure that everything fit together, that all the pieces functioned properly. If there were going to be any surprises, I'd much rather discover them in my garage than while overseas.

The wheelchairs then needed to be taken apart and grouped as individual kits. Trying to fit a hundred wheelchairs into my garage revealed a stunning fact: Unassembled wheelchairs take up far less space than assembled ones. And because they do, I knew it'd be easier to transport them, to store them, even to count them. I estimated that packaging the wheelchairs unassembled meant they'd take up less than half the space of assembled ones.

As I grouped the parts together in kits, I stacked them, one on top of the other, Tetris-style—all one hundred of them—floor to ceiling in my garage. They'd remain there for the better part of a year.

I had completed all the assignments that Skip and I had formulated in his office. I had covered all my bases, solved all the problems. Now all I needed was an opportunity, a chance to prove my point that an inexpensive, durable, functional wheelchair would be useful in the developing world.

16

THEN THERE
WERE FOUR

Irvine, California
June 2000

One Sunday morning, I was listening to a sermon at Mariners Church when suddenly I received a fierce elbow to the ribs.

"Look at this," Laurie whispered, pointing her finger at the announcement in the bulletin: *"Volunteers needed for a medical trip to India."*

"You should go," she said.

I examined the announcement. "That's only for doctors and nurses," I whispered back, trying to keep my voice down.

"Yes, but you should go with them. Give away your chairs. Try it."

I thought about it for the whole service, weighing the pros and cons. *Would they even let me go on a trip like that?* I had no medical qualifications. *How would I get my wheelchairs into the country?*

At the time, I was consulting on biometrics for Ethentica, a

117

company based in Mission Viejo, California. *Could I afford to miss two weeks of work?*

"Okay," I said to Laurie at the end of the service, "I'll go to India and try to give away my wheelchairs."

Over the following weeks, and just to be certain that I was making the right decision, I decided to seek the wisdom of some of the people in my life. On a blank sheet of paper, I created a poll with the simple question, "Should I go on the trip?" Beneath it were two options: "Yes" and "No."

The mission trip, I argued, would help me collect data for the academic paper I was working on. Having been involved in the publication of around twenty peer-reviewed articles on blood separation, artificial speech, and transdermal diagnostics for biomedical engineering journals, I thought I'd use those same skills to write a paper on the utility of wheelchairs around the world, a paper tentatively entitled "Inexpensive, Durable, Functional Wheelchair for Developing Countries."

After expressing interest in joining the mission team to India, I was informed that everyone who wanted to go had to attend meetings that were designed to brief us on the details.

About twenty-five of us came to the first meeting, which was held at Laguna Beach, a very wealthy seaside resort city in Orange County. The leader introduced himself and told us a bit of the backstory behind the trip.

Mariners Church had already sent multiple teams consisting of several dozen people to India to support a hospital in Chennai that was associated with an organization called Christian Missions Charitable Trust. The woman from New Zealand who ran the hospital had invited a team from our church to spend two weeks there in the summer to practice medicine and do some medical training for her staff.

Don Schoendorfer

Eventually, the meeting transitioned to a time of introductions. We went around the room, each of us sharing information about ourselves: our areas of expertise, why we wanted to go on the trip, that sort of thing. There were medical professionals from all different backgrounds: cardiologists, anesthesiologists, dentists, and nurses with all sorts of specialties. Then it was my turn.

"I'm Don," I said. "I'm a mechanical engineer."

"Hi, Don," the leader said. "So why are you here?"

"Because I want to bring wheelchairs to India."

"Wheelchairs?" she said. "How many do you want to take?"

"About a hundred."

The thought of bringing wheelchairs on a medical mission trip seemed like a total waste of space, especially because the need for syringes, antibiotics, stitches, and wound dressings was so high.

"And how do you plan to do that?"

"I don't know," I said. "This is my first meeting, too!"

I was determined to see it through, even as our group of prospective volunteers dwindled from twenty-five to only a handful of volunteers. Backing out wasn't an option for me. The people of India could use my wheelchairs.

Soon, though, I encountered a significant logistical quandary: How, exactly, would I get my wheelchairs to India? I needed a strategy, so I called the director of Christian Missions Charitable Trust.

"Hi, I'm Don," I said. "I'm one of the volunteers from Mariners Church coming to Chennai on this medical mission trip, and I want to bring a hundred wheelchairs with me. Can you help me figure out how to ship them there?"

"Why would you want to do that?" she asked.

"Because I want to bring wheelchairs to people in developing countries." I paused and gathered my thoughts. "All I want to do is to provide inexpensive, durable, functional wheelchairs to people in India and all around the world. And in order to make that happen, I need to collect some data to prove the legitimacy of the cause."

"Well, that's not like anything we do around here," she said.

I pressed on. "But what if I can get the wheelchairs there myself?"

She seemed open to that possibility, so as soon as we hung up, I got to work trying to figure out how to ship wheelchairs from the United States to India. Because I'd already had some experience with the shipping industry, I knew that the wheelchair kits in my garage would fill about a quarter of a shipping container. But I needed someone on the ground in Chennai, a broker of sorts who could help me orchestrate the process on the other end. I reached out to the director of Christian Missions Charitable Trust once again.

"Okay," I said, "I've got it all worked out. I can ship a hundred wheelchairs to Chennai, and I'll pay for the shipping myself. But could you give me the name of your broker? Maybe he could handle it on your end?"

On the other end of the phone, I could hear what sounded like papers on a clipboard being flipped. I held my breath and waited for her response.

"Don," she finally said, "it's not going to be possible."

"Why not?" I asked.

"Because here's the thing. Wheelchairs aren't mentioned on our list of imported exemptions. And if it's not on the list, we can't allow it into the country. If we did, we'd have big problems with our government."

Up to that point, I'd been teetering on the edge of frustration. But the director's response succeeded in pushing me over the threshold. Having spent my entire life as an engineer, having found solutions to problems others deemed impossible, the word "no" has never been part of my dictionary.

"Well, there's got to be some way around that," I told her. "I'm coming to India, and my wheelchairs are coming with me!"

I called the airline to see how much it would cost to transport a hundred wheelchairs to India by plane, and the answer made my heart sink. It would be astronomically expensive. "Okay," I said, "what if I only brought fifty wheelchairs on the plane? How much would that cost?"

That, too, would cost a small fortune, which felt like a punch to the gut. After the sobering conversation ended, I hung up the phone and went to the garage. My options had dwindled by significant numbers, just like the volunteers on our trip. I wanted to bring a hundred wheelchairs with me to India, but that number shrank to fifty, and then to thirty, and then to ten, and then, finally, to four.

I stood before the large tower of wheelchairs in my garage, struggling to come to terms with the reality. I'd only be able to bring *four* chairs to India.

17

THE TRIP

Santa Ana, California
February 2001

With the trip to India now looming, I once again glanced at the poll that I'd been tallying.

"Should I go on the trip?" That was the question. Under the "No" category, I counted twenty-eight names. Under the "Yes" category, there were thirty—a margin of only two. The people from Mariners Church were the ones who were encouraging me to go on the trip. "If God is opening a door for you," they said, "you should do it. It makes no sense, but you should go."

Out of the fifty people who first expressed interest in attending the mission trip, only three of us attended the final meeting: two nurses and me. An orthopedic surgeon named Dr. Mike Bayer also showed up. When asked why he wanted to go on the trip, Dr. Bayer said, "Because it sounds like a crazy thing to do." *We're bringing one wheelchair for each member of our team,* I realized.

The day of our departure dawned, and even before 5:00 p.m., when our flight from Los Angeles to Singapore was scheduled to depart, we began to encounter problems.

We were expected to meet one of the members of our trip at the gate at LAX. But earlier in the day, we learned that her visa to India was invalid, so she'd have to fly to San Francisco to meet with the consulate.

She arrived at the office around noon, and just as she was walking up to the counter, the representatives of the consulate shut the door. "Closed for Lunch," read the sign.

Our volunteer knew that if she didn't get her visa immediately, at that very moment, she'd miss the flight back to Los Angeles, and the whole trip would be jeopardized. She banged on the door for several minutes.

No one answered.

Meanwhile, Laurie had driven the other three of us to LAX. She wanted to celebrate the send-off with champagne and a little party, but since the church had a no-alcohol policy for mission trips, she baked us a cake and served sparkling apple juice. She never said so, but I could tell Laurie was sad to be missing the trip.

During the process of checking in for our flight, the gate attendant looked at the four wheelchairs.

"Are you planning to take these with you?" he asked.

"We are," I said.

"Sir, you can't put these wheelchairs in our baggage hold."

"What?" I asked. "Why not?"

"They're going to get damaged."

"No, they won't," I said, clanging the frame against the counter. "These are made tough."

"Sorry," he insisted. "It's against our policies. I can't let you through."

I asked to speak with his manager, who reaffirmed the airline's policy, but he also told me that if I purchased four boxes, I could stow them below the cabin with the other cargo. Even though the wheelchairs cost me about $100 to make, I went ahead and paid $125 for each box.

The plane had begun the boarding process, and still there was no sign of our fourth team member. *Is she stuck in San Francisco?* Laurie passed out the cake and juice, but all of us were on pins and needles. The itinerary had us flying from LA to Taipei, and then to Singapore, and then on to Chennai, India. *Could we go without her? Maybe she could meet us in Singapore?*

Thirty minutes till departure, and still there was no sign of her. Twenty minutes became fifteen. Fifteen became ten. I could see the plane through the airport window—the plane that had my wheelchairs stowed in its cargo hold.

Just as the flight attendant was about to close the gate, just at the very last possible minute, we saw a familiar face rushing toward us, ticket in hand.

She made it, just in the nick of time. Through all sorts of struggles and challenges, it seemed like God was still making a way for things to come together.

———————————

We landed in Singapore and met our fifth volunteer, Dr. Bayer. He'd had a successful career, performing elaborate sports shoulder surgeries. I could tell that Dr. Bayer wasn't on board with my idea.

After spending half a day in Singapore, we boarded another flight to India, which landed at 1:00 a.m.

As it was at most airports in developing countries, the immigration process in Chennai was absolute chaos. We made our way to the baggage claim area and picked up our luggage, along with the boxes of wheelchairs. Thankfully, the chairs didn't have any trouble getting through customs.

The wheelchairs weren't a problem. The boxes of medicine, though, were a different matter altogether. They'd been sent from an organization called "MAP," which was written boldly on the sides of the boxes.

The two nurses and our guide had made it successfully through customs and were waiting outside. But when the security guards saw the boxes of medication, they detained Dr. Bayer and me, questioning us and our suspicious medications.

Before the trip, our director had told us to avoid certain words that would trigger all kinds of red flags. As the security guard began his interrogation, I remembered what *not* to say, but I couldn't recall what words I actually *should* say. I was glad to be standing beside Dr. Bayer. At six foot six, he was a commanding presence.

"Where are these boxes going?" the guard asked.

"I don't remember," Dr. Bayer said, looking down at the officer.

"What do you mean, you don't remember?"

"Like I said, I don't remember."

This went on for a few minutes, back and forth, until the supervisor eventually came up and pulled out the manifest. He examined the contents and the names of all the medications, but he couldn't read English. None of the Indian officers could. And yet, when he saw the big gold embossed stamp on the sides of the boxes, his eyes went wide, as if the boxes contained something important. If he continued to hold us up, he might get in trouble with higher-ups.

"You're free to go," he said, instructing the guards to let us through.

Dr. Bayer and I exchanged a grateful glance as we joined the others outside, where a large bus was waiting to take us to the hotel.

As several men loaded our luggage through the narrow passenger door of the bus, it became clear that the wheelchairs weren't going to fit. They were going to have to store them on the roof, on some sort of rack. Without any rope to secure them, two men had to ride up there on the roof, holding the wheelchairs to keep them from sliding off. I didn't know how they were going to keep from sliding off themselves.

It was pitch dark as we traveled on the bumpy roads, twisting and turning around ridges. Every once in a while, we'd hear one of the men up on the roof let out a stifled scream, making all manner of thumping and bumping noises. I was certain that one of them would fall.

Thirty long minutes later, we arrived at the hotel, exhausted and jet lagged after thirty-six hours of travel. But after checking into our hotel rooms, all of us were thinking the same thing.

One of us walked over to the clerk sitting at the lobby desk. "Is there a place to get something cold to drink?"

"There's a club right across the driveway."

We left the hotel, crossed the street, and laughed at the club's name: Hell Freezes Over.

18

EMMANUEL

Chennai, India
February 11, 2001

Early the next day, we visited Christian Missions Charitable Trust to receive our briefing about the following day's activities. The plan was to hold a family medical clinic in a suburb of Chennai to help the local population.

During the briefing, the doctors and nurses spent their time dividing up responsibilities, assigning roles and tasks to the Indian staff who worked in the hospital. By the end of the session, I was the only person who didn't exactly know what my job would be. The focus of the group turned inevitably in my direction.

"I'm just here to give away wheelchairs," I said, showing them one of my four prototypes. I knew that behind their quizzical expressions was the same question in the minds of our team at the first mission planning meeting in Laguna Beach: *You call* that *a wheelchair?*

Missionary work, I learned, is a never-ending job. Missionaries are always running out of supplies. There are never enough resources to meet the overwhelming needs they encounter on a daily basis.

Doctors must choose which people to treat and which people not to treat. You can't save everyone. And no matter how hard you try, at the end of the day, there are always people still waiting in line, waiting for medicine and miracles.

No wonder they were skeptical. To them, my wheelchair must have looked like just another dubious idea some Westerner dreamed up for them to implement.

"Why are you here?" the Indian doctors kept asking me, suspicious of my motives.

"Because I want to write a paper," I said. "I want to prove that a wheelchair as simple as this one will have utility in your country. If it does, perhaps other organizations will become interested in providing more." From the puzzled expressions on their faces, I realized that they didn't see how this would be possible. No matter what I said, my answers didn't make sense to them, and by the end of the day, I was beginning to wonder if they made sense to me, either.

Don, what's your role here? I asked myself. *Did you make a mistake in coming on this trip?*

What can a few wheelchairs do in the face of such pain and poverty?

Early the next morning, we loaded the bus with the supplies we'd need for the "card table clinic," as they called it. Since I was an engineer and not a medical professional, my job, as it had been determined on the previous day, was to set up the tables once we arrived so that the doctors and nurses would have flat surfaces to work on.

Don, I thought, *just try not to get in their way.*

Just before we departed, I decided to bring one of the wheelchairs with me, this time secured with rope on the top of the bus—I didn't

Don Schoendorfer

want anyone else risking life and limb just to transport my chair. I pulled the rope extra tight, predicting a bumpy three-hour ride.

As we traveled toward the edge of the city, we passed by a monument dedicated to St. Thomas, one of Jesus's disciples who, according to legend, had traveled as a missionary through India and was martyred here in AD 72.

For the remainder of the ride, I thought about "Doubting" Thomas, as he was called, the most skeptical of all the disciples. I rather liked him, actually. He was a man whose faith required real evidence, a man who wouldn't believe in Jesus's resurrection without evidence—"unless I see the nail marks in his hands and put my finger where the nails were," he said (John 20:25).

I wondered what Thomas must have felt when he traveled through this part of India, so far from his home in Jerusalem. Did he feel just the way I did right then: full of doubt?

We arrived at our destination, a small village on the outskirts of Chennai. Our trip had been advertised, so the people knew to bring their families to receive medical help. Many of the locals, I was told, had never seen a doctor before.

We unloaded the supplies from the bus, and I quickly got to work setting up the card tables. The doctors and nurses unpacked their supplies, spreading out their bandages and medical equipment beneath the summer sun, which by now was tall in the sky and had caused the temperature to rise infernally high, way above a hundred degrees. It was humid, too. I looked over at the rice paddy beside us, which seemed to be a wonderful breeding ground for mosquitoes.

"Don't worry about the snakes in there," one of the Indian doctors assured me. "Not even the snakes come out when it's *this* hot."

Nothing happened for a long while. Then, we noticed two people approaching, walking toward us along the long, dirt road. As they grew closer, I could see that they were carrying something. Or someone.

It was a boy. As they grew closer, I noticed that this wasn't a boy like I'd ever seen before. He was flailing his hands and feet, shaking his head back and forth uncontrollably, grinding his teeth loudly. I'd later learn that he had cerebral palsy, a common condition in developing countries, caused by injuries during childbirth.

When there's an interruption of blood flow to a newborn, even for seconds, it can significantly affect the development of the baby's motor skills in the brain. I was told that in the slums of India, it costs three dollars to deliver a baby in a hospital. But if there aren't any hospitals near you, it might cost many times this to travel to one, which is an impossibility for many who live in developing countries. An alarming number of births are home births, often assisted by untrained birth attendants. Infant mortality is sadly common, and one out of every ten births has difficulties.

This was what likely happened to this boy who was being carried to our clinic by his parents. There was no wait, no line, so they approached one of our card tables and checked in. The boy was eleven years old, and his name was Emmanuel—a strong name in both Christianity and Hinduism.

There wasn't much for me to do since I'd already set up the card tables, so I sat in the shade next to the rice paddy and watched the doctors try to figure out how to help this young boy who was flailing. While the doctors conferred, they sent the small family back toward me.

What would happen, I wondered, *if I got that wheelchair down from on top of the bus?*

I couldn't talk to the family because I wasn't assigned a translator, and Moses, one of the guides from Christian Missions Charitable

Don Schoendorfer

Trust, was busy. So I smiled at the family and motioned for them to "just wait here." Then I climbed up on top of the bus, got the wheelchair down, and placed the chair in front of the boy.

I didn't know what to do next. With my arms, I tried communicating with them, making motions like charades, until finally the boy's mother carried over her son and lowered him into the wheelchair.

Emmanuel was shaking, swinging his arms around, and his mother kept pulling his arms and legs back into the seat. Suddenly, the boy began to calm down. His arms and legs relaxed into the white resin lawn chair, and his whole countenance changed.

His mother looked over at me, studying my face, my expression. She could see that I was happy, that she wasn't doing anything wrong, and so she started moving the wheelchair forward, making a slow series of figure eights, rolling the bicycle wheels faster across the dirt. She then directed them toward a cement platform, which had a bit of a curb. My heart began to race. *She's going to hit the curb.* I wondered if I should intervene. *This is going to be a disaster. She's going to tip over the wheelchair, the boy will fall out, and he'll get hurt!*

To my delight, she mounted the curb easily. She aimed the wheels just right, lined them up perpendicular to the edge of the curb so they'd both hit the bump simultaneously, and leaned the chair back. With the two caster wheels up, she went right over the curb and set the child down slowly onto all four wheels.

I was totally beside myself. Here was this mother, wheeling her son around like she'd been doing it for years, completely intuitively, effortlessly.

I looked over at my team members, who saw me grinning from ear to ear. It was a wake-up call for all of us, and the doctors and nurses came running over. They looked at each other in disbelief. They hadn't practiced medicine on a single person that day, yet this wheelchair was already helping the people in this remote Indian village.

The young boy likely didn't know it, but his parents were already experiencing a freedom they'd never known before.

———————

Emmanuel and his family waited at the clinic for a few hours, talking with us now through the help of a translator.

They seemed happy, but we learned that their financial situation was bleak. The family worked six days a week in a rice paddy about three miles away. If both parents were able to work, they'd be able to earn enough money to save. But caring for Emmanuel was a full-time job, and at any given time, one parent always had to be home. So they could feed themselves, their landlord allowed them to keep some of the rice they harvested.

It was a Sunday afternoon, their one day off, and when there was a pause in the medical activities, we decided to help them transport the wheelchair back to their hut, a distance of about three miles.

When we pulled into the village, we were greeted by a lot of commotion, caused by the presence of our big white bus. I did have a clipboard with me, so I started collecting some data, trying to figure out what the name of the village was. I wasn't even sure it *had* a name. It was a community located on the edge of a rice paddy: about thirty huts made of cinder blocks, corrugated metal, and baling wire. No electricity. No ventilation.

We got out of the bus and followed Emmanuel's family to their home, a room about eight by ten feet across with a dirt floor. There was a hammock with some clothes laid out. Each member of the family only owned two sets of clothes—one to wash, the other to wear. There were a few pots and pans. When it rained, they had to cook their food indoors, allowing the smoke to escape through the holes that were cut through the wall. These holes served as the only windows. Emmanuel slept in a little pen in the corner, likely to help him stay in one place. An old, torn blanket was draped over the edge of his pen.

As we were inside the hut, the neighbors began to come by. They wanted to know what was going on. We saw people hobbling on homemade crutches made of tree limbs and branches. At least two people had polio. We were asking them questions, gathering as much data as possible, and I was writing down the information on my clipboard.

There was a sense of excitement and nervousness in the room. Emmanuel was getting comfortable in his wheelchair, quite attached to it. But his parents didn't know what was going to happen. Was this just a photo op? Would we take the chair back with us? I could see the concern on their faces.

At first, I had come on this trip expecting to gather cold data, expecting just to fill in the blanks that would help me prove that my wheelchair could be useful in the developing world. Something like the following:

Name: Emmanuel

Age: 11

Condition: Cerebral palsy

Parents: Rice farmers

When I left California, this had been my expectation for this trip, to collect cold, lifeless data. But what I found instead were real people with real needs that I had the ability to meet face-to-face. I'd come to India with a paper on my mind. But I left India with people in my heart.

I felt like everything in my life had brought me to this part of the world, to this humble hut in this remote village in India, to teach me a lesson that I might not have learned if I'd stayed back in California and skipped the trip.

Don, I realized, *you don't need a fancy degree or a cutting-edge invention to make a difference in this world. You don't need fame or fortune, education, or appreciation. To create a legacy, all you need to do is love other people more than you love yourself. Lift their needs above your ambitions. Raise people up off the ground, and in doing so, you are placing them safely in the outstretched arms of a loving, protecting God.*

Suddenly, Moses rushed into the hut. "Don," he spurted, "we have to go! We have to go *right away*!"

"Why, what's up?"

"I've made a big mistake," he said. "Before coming here, I should have determined who the elder of the village was, and I should have asked him for permission to enter his village—that's the custom here, and I didn't do that." Moses wrung his hands. I could see how rattled he was, the beads of sweat on his forehead. "We've offended the elder," he said, "and he's just shown up. We need to get out of here as quickly as we can."

Just as Moses predicted, the village elder approached the hut, fuming mad, with a stern look on his face. Something told me that if we didn't leave, we were going to have a problem. Clashes between Hindus and Christians were not uncommon in this part of India.

"We really shouldn't be here," Moses kept saying, trying to rush us out of the hut.

"Okay," I said, standing firm, "but before we go, you need to do your job."

Moses looked at me in confusion.

"I'm the engineer," I said. "I did my job. Now it's your turn to do your job."

"What's my job?" he asked, frantic.

Don Schoendorfer

"Isn't that a Bible in your pocket?" I said. "I think you should tell them why we're here."

"What do you mean?"

"Moses, this is your chance to say something from the Bible. Look, I brought the wheelchair. Now you tell them why!"

With the elder of the village still enraged, Moses opened his pocket Bible, cleared his throat, and nervously began reading in Tamil, their language. I couldn't understand what he said, but whatever it was, people became very quiet and listened, even the elder. When Moses finished reading, I left the wheelchair with Emmanuel, said goodbye to his family, and made my way, along with the other doctors, back to the bus.

The bus driver was upset. We'd taken far too long making what he must have thought was an unnecessary stop, and now he wanted us to hurry. He honked his horn and hit the gas, pulling forward not even a second after the last of us was seated.

As he did, the villagers began to chase us. My American comrades looked nervous, likely thinking that we were about to be kidnapped and held for ransom. The driver didn't want to stop, so several of the men from the village maneuvered in front of the bus and placed their palms on the windshield, forcing the driver to slow to a halt. I turned around and saw Emmanuel's mother in the crowd, running toward us and carefully balancing two glasses of water.

Through our translator, I learned that it was only when she saw our bus leaving that she realized we were leaving the wheelchair for her son. Overwhelmed with gratitude, she felt she needed to give us something in exchange for what we'd given her family. All she could afford to give was water.

The drive back to Chennai took several hours, which was more than enough time to reflect on the events of the day.

Wheelchairs, I concluded, are not luxuries. They are necessities, just as much as food, water, clothes, and shelter. No human should be forced to live on the ground, no matter who you are, or where you are. Wheelchairs do more than restore mobility—they restore dignity.

My only regret was that Laurie wasn't there to share in the experience, to see Emmanuel's face as his mother rolled him around for the first time. Someone on our team had a disposable camera, so I had a couple of photos, but they were a poor rendition of such a glorious event.

But having given away my very first wheelchair—a chair that spent an entire year collecting dust in my garage—I knew it wasn't going to be the last. I'd seen with my own eyes its life-changing impact. And as we drove back to the hotel, we once again passed the monument dedicated to St. Thomas. I imagined what wheelchairs could do for the estimated millions of other people in the world like Emmanuel who need the miracle of mobility.

It was a big dream, a monumental task. But one way or another, I was going to change the world with my wheelchairs, and in doing so, demonstrate the full meaning of Emmanuel's name:

"God with us."

Don Schoendorfer

19

LOTUS BLOSSOM AND INDRA

Chennai, India
February 12, 2001

I woke up the next day feeling inspired but still somewhat unsure about what I was doing. Emmanuel seemed to really like the wheelchair, and I thought we might try giving another one away.

There wasn't a medical clinic on the schedule, so the day was wide open. Moses told me that he knew of a girl, whose name in English is "Lotus Blossom," who couldn't walk. Something in my heart convinced me to ask Dr. Bayer to accompany me.

"Hey, Mike," I said. "Maybe we could take the day off and go see if this girl is okay for the wheelchair?" I knew that I didn't have the clinical background to evaluate her, and as an orthopedic surgeon, Dr. Bayer knew far more about diagnosis and disability. I didn't want to hurt anybody with my wheelchair.

He agreed, and with the help of Moses, we drove to the place where Lotus lived, to one of the hundreds of slums in the city of Chennai.

Not all slums in India are the same. Some are beach slums, others are bridge slums or train track slums. Lotus lived in a river slum, a half acre filled with garbage just beside a festering, green river.

When we arrived, I couldn't believe my eyes. Moses led us to Lotus's thatched hut, which couldn't have been more than about ten feet from the river. I looked down at the water, horrified and repulsed at the very sight of it. There were dead animals floating belly-up in the bubbling liquid. The stench was nauseating.

We learned that Lotus's mother was what they called a "ragpicker." She spent her days rummaging through the trash, looking for food, scraps of cloth, broken glass, animal carcasses, and perhaps something to hold water—anything and everything she might be able to repurpose and sell. Every few days, another huge load of garbage was spread over the open dump, offering Lotus's mother another opportunity to scavenge.

We entered the thatched hut, stepped through the doorway. There was no floor, only dirt. And because there were no windows, everything was dark. Lotus was lying on a mat, flat on her stomach, wearing a colorful, flowing dress.

Her mother, we later learned, had been told beforehand to expect visitors who might bring Lotus a wheelchair. Wanting her daughter to look her very best for the special occasion, she'd borrowed the colorful dress from her neighbors but didn't tell Lotus we were coming, wanting to spare her daughter the disappointment in case nobody showed up.

Dr. Bayer sat Lotus up on her mat and began to examine her. I looked down at her legs. She couldn't move them at all. One of her hands was folded over on itself with no strength in the fingers. Her other arm seemed functional. I waited patiently as Dr. Bayer finished his medical evaluation, noticing how small Lotus was. It shocked me to learn that she wasn't a little girl at all. She was seventeen years old.

"She has muscular dystrophy," Dr. Bayer said, looking up at me. "I think she'd be the perfect person for a wheelchair."

I was relieved. "Okay," I said. "Pick her up and let's put her in the chair."

Dr. Bayer lifted her up, his eyes widening as he realized how light she was. Because of the muscle atrophy in her legs, she weighed about sixty pounds. He carefully settled her body into the white chair, and we rolled her outside, out of the dark hut and into the bright sunlight. She looked up at the blue sky and smiled.

Other children from the river slum were suddenly aware of our presence, aware that something unusual was going on—something with wheels. They scurried to the hut, excited by what they saw, moving rocks out of Lotus's way as her mother wheeled her around the dirt, both of them giddy. After a short stroll, Lotus suddenly became overwhelmed by all the activity happening too quickly around her, and they returned to the hut.

"I've never seen my daughter so happy," her mother said, tears streaming down her face. We helped Lotus get out of the chair and back onto her mat. Her face was still beaming from the adventure. Yet I still had grave concerns about her condition, about the slum where she lived, about the putrid river. I asked her mother if it would be possible to construct a fence between her door and the river, hopefully to prevent Lotus from accidently rolling into the water.

Six days later, when we visited the family again, the fence had been constructed.

By then, Lotus had already mastered her wheelchair. She'd use her functioning arm to push one wheel, and then switch her hand to the other wheel, propelling herself forward all by herself, slowly but independently, without anyone's help.

Before we left to rendezvous with the doctors, I looked back over my shoulder to take one final glance at Lotus. She looked so hopeful, so full of life. That same beautiful smile was still on her face.

I knew that this wheelchair had changed Lotus's life. But what I didn't know, what I had not expected, was just how much it would also change mine.

———

I wasn't totally confident about what was going to happen with our relationship with Christian Missions Charitable Trust. Before leaving California, I'd done some research of my own, hoping to find additional partners in Chennai who could share my vision for giving away wheelchairs.

I discovered a Catholic church in the area that was committed to helping the poor, not only in India but also in other developing countries. My contact was a priest named Father Winner, a man I would come to greatly admire. We were approaching the end of our mission trip, but I didn't want to leave without visiting this church. Dr. Bayer agreed to join me for the adventure, for the hour-and-a-half taxi ride, which took us through some fairly dangerous areas.

At first, Father Winner was skeptical of our intentions. He thought we might have been seeking some kind of profit with our wheelchairs. But after some time, we were able to convince him that we really did want to give them away for free. This wasn't some scheme of ours to make money. I had wanted to leave our last wheelchair with him, thinking that he might know of someone who could use it. But that didn't happen.

It all worked out, though, because we later heard back from Father Winner. He had some exciting news to share. He told us that his colleague, a man named Mr. Roy, had started an orphanage for children with disabilities. One of the children was a young girl named Indra, an orphan whose biological parents were still living but had dropped her off at the orphanage and left because they could no longer afford the cost of raising her.

Indra was extremely smart, but she wasn't given the opportunity to advance her education because she couldn't walk. And if she couldn't walk, she couldn't go to school. Mr. Roy thought she would be the perfect candidate for that wheelchair.

Just like Lotus Blossom, Indra's life was instantly changed when she received her wheelchair. She had a new attitude, a new outlook on what might be possible. Even though her legs didn't work, Indra had enough strength in her arms to get around, and with her newfound mobility, she told Father Winner that she had an important announcement to make.

Before I started giving away wheelchairs, it was impossible for me to appreciate the enormous impact that mobility can have on someone's life. To go from living your life completely on the ground, being cared for by other people, bathed and looked after by others, to suddenly receiving the freedom of motion and activity and movement—it's an absolute game changer, a life changer.

And Indra knew exactly how she wanted her life to change. "I want to go to school!" she said.

In India, if you can afford textbooks and uniforms, there are free schools where you can send your children. Indra's school, however, required qualifications. She had to show proficiency, which meant she needed resources.

"If you want to go to school, Indra," said Father Winner, "if this is something that's really on your heart, then you'll have to self-study. But we'll help you. We'll get you the materials you need."

For several months, Indra threw herself into her studies, learning as much material as she could in preparation for the qualifying exams, which she took and dropped in the orphanage's outgoing mailbox. Several weeks later, she received the exciting news: she'd passed her exams and was approved to go to school.

When the day of her orientation arrived, Indra's family, along with Father Winner and several nuns, went with her. They all arrived at 9:00 a.m., just before registration began. Indra led the way, rolling in her wheelchair, toward the building.

Father Winner knocked on the door, ready to enter. Students from inside the school were already coming outside, gathering around Indra, wondering what was going on.

"This is Indra," announced Father Winner to the registrar. "She's been accepted in this school as a student."

"Oh no," said the registrar. "There must be a mistake." She stood up, walked over to the girl in the wheelchair, and asked, "Your name is Indra?"

"Yes," Indra replied.

"I'm sorry, but you can't come to school."

"Why not?"

"Because you're in a wheelchair."

The students who overheard this conversation started making noise, whispering to each other as Indra looked up at the registrar, in full disbelief, feeling devastated.

"But I've already been accepted at this school," she said, showing her the letter.

Then Father Winner joined in, arguing with the registrar, explaining how Indra had studied the materials, passed the qualifying exams, and had already been admitted as a student. But soon, the impasse became obvious. Neither side had any intention of backing down. The nuns started praying.

The headmaster of the school came outside to see what all the commotion was about. "You're Indra?" he asked.

"Yes," she said, handing him her papers.

"And you're the one who passed this registration requirement?"

"Yes."

"Well, you see, Indra, I know you want to come to school here, and I see that you're already admitted, but we don't have the facilities to accommodate you in your wheelchair."

Indra held her ground, urgently insisting the headmaster admit her, begging and pleading with him to listen to her arguments, swaying him to see the situation through her eyes. Finally, the headmaster relented. "I've never seen someone who wants to go to school here so much," he said. Then he turned his attention to the crowd of people, to the faculty, staff, and students who were, by now, all watching.

"We're going to make some changes around here," declared the headmaster. "I'm going to move my office to the second floor, and Indra, we are going to make my office into your classroom."

Some gasped, and then everyone cheered and started clapping.

"And if you ever need to go to the second floor," the headmaster added, raising his voice above the noise, "I'm sure we can find people to carry you up the stairs."

The nuns opened their eyes, their prayers being answered. Indra was overjoyed. Her determination had paid off, and she was officially admitted into the school like all the other students.

As I listened to Father Winner recount the story of Indra and her education, my mind drifted back to the uncertainty I'd felt about coming to India in the first place. So many things had to come together to put me on that plane, to get me in that taxi.

I thought about the narrow results of my poll, the way doctors kept abandoning the mission trip meetings, the story of "The Fool's

Game," and how Laurie jabbed me in the ribs to show me the advertisement of the trip in the bulletin. Then I thought about my daughter and the important role she played in getting me to Mariners Church in the first place, the way she dragged me to the front of the stage in Phoenix and introduced me to the pastor.

To think about all the sequences of events that had to occur for Indra to receive her wheelchair—all the details working in concert together, fitting together in exactly the right time, at exactly the right place, in exactly the right way—it's impossible to even calculate it. There was a time in my life when I'd have used the word "coincidence" to describe it. But listening to Father Winner describe what became of Indra and how she used her education made me prefer the word "miracle" instead.

Indra ended up excelling at her new school. The headmaster made sure of it. Over the next few years, she progressed quickly through her education, wanting to become an artist at first, which she succeeded in doing, and then, after graduating from high school, deciding to go to college. She received her degree in computer science and began working as an architect. Then she decided to continue her education by going to graduate school, where she excelled in the field of psychology and was eventually hired as a teacher, helping students with disabilities at the same orphanage she had attended—the one that Mr. Roy had started, where her parents had dropped her off when she was a young girl.

Indra's life had come full circle, and all because of two bicycle wheels, two casters attached to a simple conduit frame, and a white resin lawn chair.

Don Schoendorfer

When I got home from India, I couldn't wait to tell Laurie about everything that happened. I told her all about Emmanuel, and Lotus Blossom, and Indra, and also about Iswari—the person to whom we ended up giving our fourth wheelchair. Laurie must have seen the emotion on my face because after I finally finished describing our experiences, she said something that took me by surprise.

With one simple sentence, Laurie summarized the entirety of my life:

"First it was blood. Then it was sweat. And now, it's going to be tears."

CHAPTER 20

ROCK BOTTOM

Santa Ana, California
February 2001

T he day after I returned from the trip to India, I got in my car and drove to work, still jet lagged. Two weeks had come and gone, and there was so much work to do.

But as I pulled into the Ethentica parking lot, I was astonished to find it empty. *That's odd*, I thought, fumbling for my keys to unlock the door to the building. I walked down the halls, noticing the absence of noise, the absence of everyone in the office except for my boss, who was at his desk, shuffling through papers.

"What happened?" I asked. "Where is everyone?"

He looked up at me, a bit surprised. "You didn't get the email?"

I felt a small panic rise up in my stomach. "No, I've been overseas without email."

"Well, Don," he said, "we went bankrupt."

Bankrupt? At first, I thought maybe he was joking. But there was too much seriousness on his face for that.

"Bankrupt?" I said. "Last I heard, you guys had $68 million worth of venture money." I paused, hoping for an explanation, wondering how in the world this happened. "I was only gone two weeks."

As it turned out, the company had burned through their entire funds trying to develop a market for biometric identification that just wasn't there. They had been waiting for a knight in shining armor to save them from financial ruin, but that knight never came. All the money was gone.

"We want you to stick around," he said, to my relief. "We need the brains to stay because that's who they'll want to invest in."

I lingered at that company for about three months. They paid me, of course, until even those last prospects ran out. That's when, for the first time in my career, I found myself out of a job. In one of the lowest moments of my life, a moment that marked the end of so many of my professional dreams, I sat down at the computer and filed for unemployment.

This isn't how this was supposed to be, I thought. *This isn't what my life was supposed to look like.*

Life was about to hit rock bottom. Laurie and I had some savings, but medical insurance was going to be a big problem. I needed a job, and I needed one fast. With my MIT degree and work experience, I did manage to pick up a few consulting jobs here and there, enough to cover the bills, at the very least. Between those gigs and the unemployment benefits, we were surviving, but barely.

Meanwhile, the volunteers who traveled with me to India had begun sharing some of our experiences at Mariners Church, talking about the success of the first few wheelchairs we gave away. In a church that big, word spread quickly. My phone began to ring.

"What are you going to do next?" they'd ask.

"Well, I've got to find a job."

"Why don't you work on wheelchairs?" That was the common refrain among my church friends, almost as if it was obvious to everyone except me. Some said it gently, subtly, mentioning it like a question that had just dawned on them. Others were bolder about it.

"Can't you see how God is working in your life?" they'd ask straightforwardly. "Don't you understand why all this is happening?"

I didn't understand. At least, not yet. My main interest was in proving that the wheelchair idea would work, not in making a new career out of it. This was a side project, not a professional venture. I'd leave that for someone else to pick up.

But they persisted. "Do you really think you did this on your own? Do you think all of this is just coincidental?"

No was the answer. I hadn't done this alone, and I didn't think it was coincidental, not anymore. The more I spoke with members of the church, the more I became aware that my mindset was shifting. Conversation after conversation, I began to consider their arguments more seriously.

Maybe I should give some thought to this wheelchair thing.

But there was still the matter of income. Our savings were dwindling so low that I could almost see the bottom. Like my former company, I had also run out of financial options and needed a knight in shining armor to come to my rescue.

Then, one Saturday morning, as Laurie and I were sitting at the kitchen table, she looked over at me with a determined expression on her face. I knew she was about to tell me something that she'd been thinking about for quite some time.

"Don," she said, "you need to focus on this wheelchair idea of yours. You've let me stay home for sixteen years to fulfill my dream of looking after our girls. Now, it's my turn to go back to work and support the family so that you can do this."

By Monday, Laurie had secured a job with the Social Security Administration, her first job since working as the Deputy Regional Commissioner in Boston years earlier. With all the experience she'd marshaled over the years, she was overqualified for the position, but they hired her back as a claims representative, the same position she'd begun the day she graduated from college forty years earlier.

It was a situation that could have been humiliating for many people, but I knew that it wouldn't take long for Laurie's colleagues to see the depths of her understanding and leadership skills. She'd be promoted soon and often, I knew, just like in Boston. Her new position came with a very modest salary, but it was a job. It meant that we didn't have to sell our house or move our family, and more importantly, it came with medical insurance.

Because of Laurie, I was able to focus exclusively on developing the wheelchair idea. She gave me the confidence and support to take that leap of faith, and I put all my time and energy into revising my original blueprints and improving on the work I'd done.

This came just in time, too: during those depressing months of unemployment, I felt that all of my hard work and expertise had been for nothing. I felt like I'd wasted my life, my PhD, my career, my expertise. I didn't think I'd ever be satisfied working outside the academic world of cutting-edge research, away from the resources that had been my safety net, away from the front lines of invention and technology. Then, the phone rang.

"Hey, Don," a voice on the other line said. "It's Jim, and I want to send you a check."

It took me a few seconds to ask my friend from church the obvious question: "Why? What do you want to send me a check for?"

"I want you to get more wheelchairs."

More wheelchairs? "I don't have room for any more wheelchairs," I explained. "I still have ninety-six of them in my garage."

Don Schoendorfer

"Don," he said, "you need to start a nonprofit."

Within days of that unexpected conversation, a check arrived in the mail, made out to me personally. *What am I supposed to do with this?*

And then it happened again. Another check arrived in the mail. And then another. Before long, I knew I needed to figure out what to do with all this money. I asked Mariners Church if they'd consider accepting the checks, keeping them in an account earmarked for the wheelchairs. They agreed.

As more checks rolled in, the idea of starting a nonprofit took root in my mind, comically at first. In a way, I was more than qualified to start a nonprofit. *I know a lot about not making a profit,* I thought.

The first thing on the agenda was to buy a copy of *Nonprofit Kit for Dummies*. The title was fitting because I certainly felt like a dummy. According to the book, the first thing I needed was to set up a 501(c)(3). I searched around, found an attorney in Michigan who said he could get me one for $1,500, and filled out the forms.

The next chapter of the *Dummies* book said I needed a board. *But who?*

"Laurie," I asked, "do you want to be on the board?"

She agreed. I then asked Dr. Bayer, Skip Lanfried, Karen Taulien (who had organized our trip to India), and Karen Wilson, with whom I'd worked closely in my earlier efforts to tutor and mentor adolescents at the church.

Okay, I thought, *we have a board! What's next?*

I flipped to the next chapter.

Looks like we need bylaws and a meeting. I opened my calendar and scheduled the first board meeting for September 10, 2001.

By that time, as I was trying to structure the nonprofit, I was also keenly aware that I'd only given away *four* wheelchairs. There were still ninety-six sitting in my garage. I had to find something to do with them.

Also, I'd long given up hope of writing my academic paper. With all the enthusiasm and funds coming in from church members, it was obvious that I didn't need clinical data to prove that the wheelchairs were effective. The stories were coming back to us from India—stories of individuals, families, and entire communities that were radically impacted by the simple gift of a wheelchair. Those stories communicated more powerfully the legitimacy of our endeavors than an academic paper ever could.

Soon, because of all the generous checks that were coming in, I had received enough money to distribute my remaining wheelchairs. Mariners Church connected me with a group in Chicago who agreed to ship half of my wheelchairs to Angola. I had to call Dr. Bayer to let him know the good news.

"Mike," I said, "I'm going to Angola."

"What are you going to do there?"

"I've sent these forty-three wheelchairs there, and I want to go and get some stories about them. I need to come back with something I can show people so that they can understand what I'm doing."

"Well," said Dr. Bayer, "you're not going to Angola by yourself. I'm going with you."

When another man from the church, a gifted cinematographer named Glen Owen, agreed to go with us to document the trip, I felt that everything was coming together swiftly, albeit a little unexpectedly.

As the trip approached, I took a step back to get some perspective on this new season of life. I had the beginnings of a nonprofit, a board, a board meeting, and enough funds to ship half of my remaining wheelchairs to another continent. With the doldrums of unemployment behind me, and the skies above me full of promise, I turned all my attention to Africa, eager to catch the next wave that would mark the beginning of another great adventure.

21

NEVER ENOUGH

Angola
December 2001

A few weeks later, we landed in Angola. From the window of the airplane, you'd think Luanda, its capital, was a vacation resort, with its long, sandy beaches stretching out to greet the deep turquoise waters of the Atlantic. But for nearly two and a half decades, ever since Angola gained its freedom from Portugal, the country had been ravaged by civil war, forcing millions of families to flee their homes, littering its fields and towns with land mines and explosives.

We were greeted at the airport by Jose, our host, who drove us to our first destination, a large distribution center. As we unloaded the first four assembled wheelchairs from the back of a van, something nearby caught my eye. It was a large, dark-green army tent that the Angolan government had set up to house people with disabilities, a place to put them.

Suddenly, I saw two men emerge from the tent, both having lost mobility due to polio. They were dragging themselves across the dusty gravel, each using their hands and one of them using a metal pipe. I couldn't believe how fast these guys were moving, scooting at almost jog-like speed. When they got closer, I could see how torn up their hands and knees were, how scabbed and scarred. I looked over at Dr. Bayer. We were thrilled to give them the wheelchairs.

As I bent down to make some modifications, the first man reached up and grabbed hold of the chair, stabilizing it with his strong arms so I could tighten the bolts even faster. He looked so motivated, so determined to help me. From the look in his eyes, I knew he was hoping that *this* chair would belong to him.

I set the chair upright on its wheels, having made the final adjustments. And not a second later, the man propelled himself into its seat, using his powerful arms to jump. The swiftness of his movement caught me off guard. When the next wheelchair was ready, the second man did the same thing. With his one strong arm, he spun himself around on the ground, doing a complete 180-degree turn without even straining, then lunged up into the lap of the chair.

Dr. Bayer and I watched the two men settle into their new wheelchairs. They were smiling at each other, laughing and zipping around, celebrating the moment. For what may have been the first time in their lives, they were up off the ground. Their faces shone with gratitude and amazement.

We still had two more chairs to give away, but it didn't look like anyone else was coming, so we decided to go ahead and load them back into the van. But just then, we heard a strange noise, a muffled sound in the distance that was growing louder, coming closer. We stopped loading the chairs and walked around the vehicle to see what all the commotion was.

A massive wave of people was coming toward us, dragging themselves on the ground as fast as their arms could carry them. Evidently, word had spread in the nearby area that we were giving away wheel-chairs. I scanned the crowd, counting about seventy people who were making a beeline for our position, urgently trying to reach us. I couldn't believe my eyes. And neither could Glen, our cinema-tographer, who climbed up on top of the van to capture the scene.

"Don, we don't have enough wheelchairs," Dr. Bayer said. "What do we do?"

I didn't know, exactly.

The need was so great, and we only had two more chairs to give away. I knew they'd probably end up sharing the wheelchairs anyway. "Maybe we give them to the first people who arrive," I said, trying to think of the fairest thing to do.

So that's what we did: we presented the last two wheelchairs to the two men who had fought hardest to get to our van. More and more people were approaching, swarming around us as we adjusted the chairs to fit their bodies.

We had run out of chairs to give away, but the crowd continued to come toward us. Jose did his best to calm them down, explaining that we'd run out of the four wheelchairs we'd brought, but that we'd be sure to return to give them more. We watched their faces fall as they processed the devastating news. *Sure, you'll be back,* I imagined them thinking. *We've heard that before.*

Then another wave of people arrived, and Jose had to explain the same thing to them, promising wheelchairs for each of them. Over and over this happened, wave after wave, until the crowd began to disperse, crawling away from us in the wake of the four men who were racing toward the tent in their new wheelchairs.

Then my eyes came to rest on the last person who reached us, a woman. She had been at the back of the crowd, moving slowly across the ground in a zigzag manner. It was obvious to me that she'd lost her eyesight. She'd extend her arms way out in front of her, feeling for obstacles to avoid, and then cautiously scoot a few feet before reaching out again. I assumed she'd also lost her hearing. Even with Jose only a few feet away, her face still had some hope on it, still some excitement.

A wave of guilt swept over me. I looked over at Dr. Bayer, who was also having a crisis of conscience. *Should we try to take the wheelchair away from the first man and give it to this woman instead? Maybe I'd made the wrong decision. Maybe we should have given the chairs to the last people who arrived, not to the first.*

I couldn't take it anymore.

"Jose," I said, looking at the woman and also at the lingering crowd gathered around her, "we can't just leave these people. We've got to get more chairs here."

"We've already promised these wheelchairs to other people," he said. "We've already made plans for them."

"Well, there's got to be another way. We've gotta have more options here," I said, racking my brain. "What do you need? Money?" I ran my hand through my hair, pulling back a wet hand. "How much money do you need?

"Sit down," Jose said strictly, gesturing toward the back of the van. "Let me tell you a little thing about what it's like to be a missionary."

I was startled by his tone but did what he said, keeping my eye on the woman on the ground.

"You are never going to have enough to meet the need," Jose said, looking at me squarely, intently, pausing to let those words sink in.

You are never going to have enough.

"And if you let it get to you, Don," he said, "you'll quit. Every day, you'll go home wishing you had more." He looked over at Dr. Bayer, who was now also listening.

"And if you're not cut out for it," Jose concluded, "then you probably need to think about what you want to do for your future. This is just the way it is. You are never going to have enough."

———————————

I was feeling sick to my stomach, having to leave the crowd like that, having to abandon the woman on the ground as Jose ignited the engine and drove us back through the city. I watched them disappear as we pulled away from the government camp, sitting silently, still processing everything I'd seen.

On the drive back, we passed by a prestigious part of Luanda, a wealthy portion of the city that had a beautiful, gated community. It looked like something you'd see in the wealthiest parts of California.

"That's where all the expatriates live," Jose explained, telling us a bit about the history of the city. He told us about Angola's checkered past, how the oil-rich country had gained independence, how the gold and diamond mines had brought wealth to the Russians who kept fostering a civil war so they could exploit the natural resources.

"As a boy," he said, "when you reach a certain age, you go to war. Everyone does."

I was surprised to learn that there was only one man for every ten women in Angola, and that the men who survived worked as guards for gas stations and drugstores.

I wanted to thank Jose and his family for hosting us, so I'd promised to make everyone pizza that evening—one of the few things that I am actually capable of cooking with a fair amount of pride. It took us about two hours to assemble the ingredients. We found the tomato sauce at one grocery store, the cheese at another. And Jose was right. Everywhere we went, at every entrance, there were men armed to the teeth, holding machine guns and ammunition. "It's what keeps the peace around here," Jose said.

We finally arrived at our destination: Jose's apartment. But as we pulled into the crowded parking lot, just as Jose squeezed the van into a spot, I saw a huge fistfight break out. A few cars away, men were punching each other, literally beating each other up to fight for the few remaining places to park their vehicles.

Jose quickly led us through them, avoiding a confrontation, and took us to his apartment, eight stories up. As we entered the modest apartment, he introduced us to his wife, a charming lady, and also to his two sons, whom we found working in the lab in the back, a place where Jose trained people to use computers.

As I was in the kitchen, preparing the pizza, we got to know the family better. They were a highly educated family, all of them fluent in English. Jose told us about his brothers and sisters back home in Portugal, how successful they were. Some of his siblings had moved their families to Brazil, living in countries where Portuguese was the language, working as doctors and lawyers.

As Jose continued talking about his family, my eyes drifted over to Dr. Bayer, who was sitting quietly, listening intently. I could tell something was on his mind, something that was disturbing him.

"Jose," I overheard him say with a blunt tone, "I don't understand why you live in this poor country."

Jose stopped talking, a bit startled by the interruption.

"Look, you've got kids here," he continued. "And there's a fistfight happening downstairs. I know you're an intelligent guy, and your family's intelligent. You've gotta get out of here. This place is a dump!"

Oh no. Mike's gone rogue.

"If you feel like you really want to help the community," he added, "go help the community and bring some money back."

I put down whatever I was holding in my hand to watch the reaction of our gracious host. Jose waited a few seconds, then stood up, walked to the other side of the room, grabbed a newspaper, and returned to the living room. I abandoned the pizza and joined them.

"Mike," he said, "what do you see in this picture?"

Dr. Bayer looked down at the open newspaper. I could see it, too. There was a photograph of fifty or sixty men from Angola standing next to each other. "What do you see in this picture?" Jose asked again.

Dr. Bayer didn't say a word.

"Do you know what I see?" Jose said. "I see my brothers and sisters. I can't leave them." Then Jose pointed to the back of his apartment. "And you see those two kids using the computers in the other room? My sons?"

Dr. Bayer nodded silently.

"Well, I'm not going to make a huge difference in my society all by myself. It's going to take a lot longer. But if I can raise those two kids right, *they* will make a difference. So I can't leave, you see. I *won't* leave."

After that, the evening unfolded rather uneventfully. And so did the next few days when we returned to distribute the remaining wheelchairs. Glen was able to secure enough good camera footage so we could return from our trip with something to show for our work, but for the entire flight home, all I could think about were those people on the ground, crawling toward us on their hands and knees, moving as fast as they could toward our van. I thought about that woman, the way she so desperately needed a wheelchair, the hope that lingered on her face long after everyone else had turned away, disappointed.

Most of all, though, I thought about Jose's determination to stay in Angola, and his desire to leave a legacy in this country through his children. Those were the kinds of words that keep you up at night. And so were the words he shared with me.

You are never going to have enough.

22

NONPROFIT FOR DUMMIES

Irvine, California
April 2002

When we arrived back home, Glen edited the camera footage that he'd taken from our trip to Angola, and we showed it to a few people. It was an emotional video that was never met with dry eyes. Every time I watched it, I also teared up, feeling helpless to meet the overwhelming demands for wheelchairs, but more motivated than ever to try. I realized that I needed to expand my vision, to dream bigger, to increase the size and scope of my faith.

I made contact with another group, this one in North Carolina, who agreed to ship my remaining forty-three wheelchairs to India.

Around that time, we also hammered out a formal name for our organization. We tossed around several names, but none of them stuck. Our name needed to be simple. And it needed to echo the heartbeat of our *mission*: to give away *free wheelchairs*.

Free Wheelchair Mission.

This name, we believed, would best help us communicate to the world our values. We wanted to give our wheelchairs away for *free*. There was never a desire to sell them, even inexpensively. Besides, the people who most desperately needed our chairs could never afford them, even at discounted rates.

The *mission* part of our name also represented an essential strand of our DNA. We would not be a secular or merely humanitarian organization. Even though we'd be interacting with a wide range of secular and religious traditions around the world, we wanted to be a faith-based organization, a Christian organization, drawing the markers of our identity around the person and work of Jesus— following His example in showing compassion and mercy to the world, and especially to the poor, the sick, and those living with disabilities. But at the same time, we didn't want to be affiliated with any one specific denomination, flavor, or "brand" of church. Nor did we want to deny wheelchairs to anyone based on race, ethnicity, gender, or religion.

With that in mind, having crystalized our identity, having hammered out our name, it was now time to share the story of Free Wheelchair Mission in a public way, in an event scheduled for April of 2001.

I was introduced to Bob Shank, who had started an organization called the Barnabas Group, a place where business leaders could connect with ministry opportunities. They were hosting their second meeting at the Santa Ana Country Club, and I was scheduled to be one of the speakers.

There wasn't much time to prepare.

Our team quickly pulled together a video that I could show, finishing it the evening before the event. The video was on VHS, so I needed to bring a VHS player with me. I also needed to bring something to play my PowerPoint presentation. I didn't own a laptop, so I ended up walking through the doors of the Santa Ana Country Club with a VCR and my desktop computer in my arms. I lugged the cumbersome equipment into the room and set it up, and before long, it was my turn to speak.

"I'm just here to tell you the story of what we're doing," I said. "And I hope you get excited about it." I asked for a volunteer, someone who'd be willing to crawl across the stage. One man volunteered, and he began crawling on his hands and knees toward me. "What do you see?" I asked when he came near.

"Just legs," he said.

"And how do you feel down there?"

"Pretty helpless."

Then I showed a video that captured some of the moments from our trips. It was short, only a few minutes long, but before I even had a chance to give my personal explanation of our mission, I heard a voice calling out from the back of the room.

"What does your ministry need?"

"Everything," I said.

Then came another voice: "Do you have a strategic plan?"

Truncating the rest of my presentation, I decided to open the floor for questions. "Ask me anything," I said.

"Do you want me to help you compose a strategic plan?" said someone else, a man named Bret Trowbridge.

"Sure, okay," I blurted out, not knowing exactly what the offer would entail. Then another person chimed in.

"Do you have any public relations material?"

I didn't know what that meant exactly, but I accepted his offer to help me develop some.

"How much would a container of wheelchairs cost?" asked another.

It was a good question, and I didn't have an answer for it. "Um, I'll have to get back to you on that," I said.

The meeting ended, and after exchanging contact information with several people who had attended, I walked out of the country club, toting my desktop computer and VHS player to the car, wires dragging in my wake. On the way home, I began calculating the cost of shipping an entire container of wheelchairs, eventually arriving at the number: $25,000. I sent that information to the businessman. A few days later, I received a check from him for the full amount.

Then a new problem dawned on me. *Where on earth am I going to get enough wheelchairs to fill an entire shipping container?*

In a process that took more than six weeks and hundreds of hours of meetings, we developed a strategic plan: to provide twenty million wheelchairs by 2010, which was only nine years away.

It was a God-sized goal, a "big, hairy, audacious goal" that would stretch our resources and force us to grow.

"Twenty million?" people would ask. "Really? How many wheelchairs have you made so far?"

"A hundred," I'd say.

No one thought the plan was possible, but everyone wanted to see us try, so they kept giving us money.

One of the things I've discovered about myself over the years is that I'm good at telling a story, but I'm absolutely terrible, perhaps even miserable, at closing a deal. "Don," someone said at our first fundraising attempt, "aren't you going to ask for money?"

"I wasn't planning on it," I said, "but now that you mention it . . . "

I knew I had to remedy this shortcoming, so I signed up to take a course on fundraising through the University of California.

Meanwhile, as Laurie and I shared the story of Free Wheelchair Mission, the money kept coming in. People kept approaching us, curious about what we were doing, excited to figure out how they could help us. As we met new people with a variety of talents and gifts, our board continued to grow. It felt as though God was sending us the right people at just the right time, though sometimes in the most unexpected ways.

On one occasion, I was doing a radio announcement on a local Christian broadcasting station in Los Angeles. The host of the show asked me a question about finances, about our accounting.

"We're trying our best," I said.

There was a man listening to that radio broadcast on that particular day. I'd never met him before in my life, but soon, Denny Kromer became our CFO.

When I tutored through our church's Learning Center, I was introduced to a man named Randy Bergstedt. Little did I know how significant that relationship would be.

Randy and I tutored together on Tuesday afternoons, each of us assigned to a different group of students. But because of Randy's schedule, his availability was sporadic. When he was forced to miss a session, I covered for him, absorbing the kids from his group into my own. I didn't mind. After all, I wasn't a great tutor, and none of it was going very well, so a few extra students certainly weren't going to mess things up.

One Tuesday, after Randy returned from one of his hiatuses, my curiosity got the best of me. "Where do you go?" I asked him. "On the days you don't come here, where do you go?"

"I work for Star Trac Fitness," he said. "I have to travel to Taiwan often to work on a new product development project."

I know that company, I thought. *Don't they sell exercise equipment?* An idea began to form in my mind.

"You make stationary bicycles, right?" I asked.

Randy nodded.

"So do you think your manufacturer could make a wheelchair?"

Randy pulled a business card from his wallet and said, "This is the vice president of marketing for the group we work with in Taiwan."

I looked at the card he handed me.

"She speaks excellent English and lives in Vancouver," Randy said. "Give her a call or send her an email. Let's see what happens."

The next day, I called and explained the idea behind Free Wheelchair Mission and asked Randy's contact if she could produce wheelchairs for me.

"I'm going to be down in Santa Barbara tomorrow," she said. "Why don't you drive up so we can talk? Can you bring a sample with you?"

I still had a couple of wheelchairs in my garage, so the next day, I loaded them up and took them to the hotel where she was staying. After seeing the chairs and hearing about my vision, she gave me some great news.

"I'm confident I can find a manufacturer for you," she said. "Go ahead and box up one of your wheelchairs and send it to us. We'll pay for the shipping."

I got home, packaged up a wheelchair, and sent the huge box—the size of a washing machine—to Taiwan. From there, she sent it to a group of manufacturers in Shenzhen, China, which happened to be one of the bicycle manufacturing capitals of the world.

In about a week, they sent me photos of a prototype. The chair wasn't exactly white, and it was much smaller than I'd expected, but the company said they could manufacture the chairs for under $30 each.

That price was a cause for celebration. But there were problems with the chair. For one, it wasn't very stable. With hardly any effort, you could tip it over backward.

"You've got to make it stable," I explained. "You've got to make it so that it can go up a ramp."

Soon, the bicycle manufacturers discovered what I had also discovered, that nothing could be as affordable and stable as the white resin lawn chairs. They added it to the prototype, which fixed the instability problem.

One day, I received a phone call from them. "We're ready to make you a full container of wheelchairs," they said. "Where should we send it?"

Our board decided that it was best for the container to be shipped to us in California so that we could distribute the wheelchairs throughout Mexico and in South America.

The wheelchairs didn't have footrests or brakes. They didn't have push handles either. They were basically a lawn chair with four wheels, just like my old prototype. But they rolled, and they didn't tip over, and that's what mattered most.

Meanwhile, one of the members of our church, Stuart Rattray, had been looking for something to do outside of his career, something he could do to help other people. He learned about my wheelchairs and introduced himself. It was a fortuitous meeting. As it turned out, Stuart had decades of leadership experience in global shipping companies. Also, because of his worldwide contacts, he was able to make the right connections for shipping many of our containers in the following years—yet another sign that God's hand was guiding the trajectory of our mission.

In the first year of Free Wheelchair Mission, we gave away my first hundred wheelchairs. A little more than a year later, we'd given away twenty-four thousand.

23

THE KING OF GHANA

Irvine, California
July 2004

O ur first large fundraiser was fast approaching, an event on a much larger scale than anything we'd ever attempted. We hoped it would allow us to raise some significant money, and I knew we needed a great public speaker, someone who could draw a crowd, hold their attention, and share our vision. The problem was, I couldn't find anyone. My only contacts were the members on our board of directors.

So, at our next board meeting, I cast the vision to the group, hoping for a miracle.

One gentleman spoke up. Several months earlier, he'd traveled to Ghana and met the king of one of the traditional chiefdoms. "You're always bragging about your connections in Ghana," one of the other board members goaded him. "Why don't you invite the king of Ghana to speak!"

He took this as a personal challenge. And as it turned out, he succeeded. King Otumfuo Osei Tutu II of the Empire of Asante was scheduled to speak at our fundraising event.

––––––––––––

The night before the event, the king and "Mrs. King," as she was known in Ghana, joined the other out-of-towners at my house for a welcome party and some homemade American pizza.

I walked outside to see three black Suburbans pull up, complete with an entire entourage of traditionally dressed guests. After formal introductions were made, I invited them into my home, encouraging them to make themselves comfortable. One of the king's men put a pillow in one of our outside chairs, ensuring he would be sufficiently elevated before he sat down. Another cooled him with an ornate fan.

"So," I said, trying to break the ice while waiting for the pizzas to cook, "tell me a little bit about your journey to becoming a king."

"I was born in Ghana," the king said. "My father was the king. But my brother was the next oldest. So when my father died, he became the king. I wanted my children to be educated in North America, so we moved from Africa to Toronto, Canada, where I was a senior consultant at the Mutual of Omaha Insurance Company. I returned to Ghana in 1989 to start a transport business, and one day, I received a call from the secretary of state of Ghana. 'I have good news and bad news,' the man told me. 'The bad news is that your brother has just died. But the good news is that you are now the king.'"

I listened with rapt attention.

"I had no knowledge of how to be king," he explained. "I was very happy selling insurance in North America, and then with my transport business in Ghana. We had a house, a neighborhood, a family, children. But now I had to learn to be a king."

He described what being a king in Ghana entailed, a process that took about three years to learn. He was no longer allowed to eat in public, which, he explained, was why he had to politely decline the offer of my pizza.

As the evening went on, though, I could see that he was growing hungry, even famished. I really wanted the king of Ghana to eat, so I suggested that the other guests turn their backs for a moment, which they did, as the king enjoyed the first slice of American pizza he'd eaten in a long time. The evening turned out to be an enjoyable success for everyone, an event that our neighbors who attended still talk about—that time when the king of Ghana came to visit Don.

"I'm looking forward to speaking tomorrow," the king said, just before leaving our home. "I'm looking forward to getting up to tell people what they should be doing with their money."

Nobody knew what the king was going to say—not me, not any of the board members, not even our board member, his contact. Everyone on the board was still surprised that he'd even accepted our speaking request.

The next evening, we gathered for our fundraiser event. There must have been about 250 people there, many of them generous donors and those who had purchased items for our silent auction. When it was the king's turn to speak, I watched him walk up onto the stage. *What is he going to tell them about how they should spend their money?*

"Here you are living in America," he began, addressing the audience. "And you don't even know how much life you have left." The seriousness of his tone caused me to feel anxious. *Did we make a mistake in inviting him?*

Then the king smiled and said, "You're very blessed." He gestured down at his clothing. "And yes, I am a king, so I dress like this."

Everyone laughed.

"But there are people dying in my country because they do not have food to eat." He paused, scanning the crowd, taking his time. The silence was deafening.

"Do you hear God speaking to you? Right now, don't you think there is a reason for you to be here? Shouldn't you be doing something more with the blessings God gave you?"

Something about his words struck a chord in me. That was the same question I felt God had once asked me. *Don, isn't there something more that you can do for my kingdom?*

By the time the king of Ghana finished speaking, the room was moved to tears. An unexpected sequence of events had brought us an unexpected speaker with an unexpected message. But maybe that's how God likes to get His work done: unexpectedly.

That night, we raised a quarter of a million dollars.

24

OVERWHELMING NUMBERS

Lima, Peru
September 2004

Robert Barriger, a pastor in Lima, Peru, was thrilled to receive word that we were shipping him an early container of wheelchairs—550 chairs in total—that he could distribute in his community. He designated one hundred of the chairs to be given away in Surco, a small suburb of Lima.

It was going to be a monumental event for the community and the church, one that would attract the local mayors and the media. A huge stage was constructed for the event and "Free Wheelchairs" were advertised all around the city.

On the morning of the distribution, Robert and the city officials who were slated to spearhead the event climbed up onto the stage. In the distance, they saw a wave of humanity moving toward them.

Some were crawling on their hands and feet. Others were carried in the arms and on the backs of friends and family members. Some dragged themselves across the ground with their arms, and others scooted on their backs, wriggling their way along the dirt.

In all, more than six thousand people would show up, hoping to receive the one hundred wheelchairs. The mayor realized what was happening and quickly handed the microphone to the pastor to explain.

"I'm so sorry," Robert said. "We're going to get more wheelchairs for you. You will have a wheelchair. Please, please don't give up your faith in God."

———————————

We had a rubric that we used to calculate the number of wheelchairs needed in any developing country: approximately 2 percent of the population. In war-torn countries, or in places where the environment is toxic and people are often born with congenital conditions, that percentage could be higher. But generally, about 2 percent of the population needs wheelchairs.

I soon began taking mission trips to different countries, sizing up the need for chairs and figuring out the logistics for getting them there. Laurie came with me on many of these trips, and we often brought supporters who were up for this sort of adventure. One of those trips—an unforgettable one—took us to Armenia.

Armenia had a population of three million people, which meant that 60,000 people needed mobility. But according to Armenia's Ministry of Health, that number was much lower. The Minister of Health claimed that there were only 538 people in her country who needed wheelchairs.

"That's remarkable," I said to her.

"Why do you say that?" she asked.

"Well, this number is remarkably low, based on what I've heard from other developing countries. If it's true, congratulations to you!"

I knew she was wrong about the need for wheelchairs, so we decided to send a container of 550 anyway. Not long after the container arrived, Laurie and I brought a team of supporters with us to help with the distribution.

We walked into the modest home of a young girl named Julia, who was about eight or nine years old. Because of her cerebral palsy, the government had identified Julia as disabled. She lived with her mother and grandmother. Years earlier, her father had left the family to take a job in Moscow. He never returned.

Laurie and I found Julia lying in a bed, cuddling a teddy bear beneath a quilt. As soon as we walked through the door of her room, she quickly turned her head toward the wall, away from us.

"These people are here to give you a wheelchair," her mother said, trying to get Julia to cooperate, but the bashful girl wouldn't budge.

We had the wheelchair with us, but we needed to figure out how to get Julia out of the bed and into it so that I could make some adjustments.

Her mother finally maneuvered Julia so that she was sitting on the edge of her bed, then picked her up and placed her into the chair. I identified the adjustments we needed to make and helped move her back into the bed. Julia pulled the quilt up to her neck and turned back toward the wall with her teddy bear as her mother looked over at me, embarrassed.

When I finished adjusting the chair, I looked back at Julia, trying to make eye contact. We needed to get her back into the chair to make sure it fit her. Suddenly, I remembered that I'd brought a camera with me. I pulled it out and began performing an elaborate show for her, goofing around with it, making funny noises and falling over.

It worked. *She's looking at me now.* As I helped her back into the chair, I could feel that she had some strength in her hands and her arms. Finally, I got the footrest adjusted and asked, with the help of her mother, who translated, "Are you comfortable?"

"I am comfortable," Julia said.

"Okay," I said. "Now Julia, I want you to squeeze my hands as tightly as you can."

She curled her small hands around mine.

"Ouch!" I exclaimed, smiling at her. "You have quite a bit of strength!" Julia grinned back at me.

"Okay," I continued, "I want you to push on my hand as hard as you can . . . now pull on it . . . good. Now the other arm." Despite her condition, Julia still had enough strength in her arms to push the wheelchair, which was a great sign.

"Okay, Julia," I said, "we're going to do a test." I could see that she was nervous. "I want you to put your hand on the wheel and push forward as hard as you can. Push the wheels away from you."

The wheels of the chair were resting on carpet—not the easiest material to propel a wheelchair over—but Julia managed to push the wheel, slowly at first. It moved. Julia's face lit up, utterly amazed at what she'd done.

This is probably the first time she's ever moved voluntarily in her entire life, I thought.

"You can do it again," I encouraged her. "And you can pull the wheel back, too!"

She pushed and pulled the wheel, getting more excited with every movement.

"Now, let me show you how to turn," I said. I kept one wheel still while pushing the other one forward. She emulated my movements, turning the chair on her own, without anyone's help. And as she did,

Julia became a totally different person. The bashful, sullen child I had met upon our arrival had transformed into a gleefully independent one who was smiling and laughing.

"Hey, Julia," I said, "come over to the window."

She wheeled over to the window where I was standing and followed my gaze, looking through the pane of glass. "What do you see out there?" I asked.

In the distance was a mountain, the very one where Noah's ark had landed in the book of Genesis.

"I see Mount Ararat," Julia said.

"How would you like to go there?" I could see on her confused face that my question had challenged her. "You know you can go there now, to that mountain, because you have this wheelchair."

A huge grin stretched across her young face. And in that instant, I saw hope come alive in her eyes. After being cooped up in her cramped room with only her teddy bear for so long, Julia realized that there was a new world awaiting her, a world that, once upon a time, she had first seen in the mountain rising up outside her bedroom window.

25

THE OVAL OFFICE

Irvine, California
August 2005

By 2005, Free Wheelchair Mission had distributed more than one hundred thousand wheelchairs across the world. Much of my work involved traveling, but I also spent quite a bit of time at my office desk, working through the lunch hour, losing track of time. In the early days, my typical lunch consisted of Diet Coke and baby carrots. I'd fill my mouth full of carrots and then let the Diet Coke wash it all down. It wasn't a quick process, as you can imagine.

One afternoon, I'd settled in at my desk and had my mouth just about packed full of carrots when my phone rang. I listened for a few moments, hoping someone else would answer the call, but no one did. I picked up the receiver and mumbled, "Hello?"

The voice on the other line introduced herself as Catherine and said she was calling from the White House.

Yeah, right, I thought. This *is exactly the kind of prank my friend Catherine would pull.* I made a futile attempt to wash down my mouthful of carrots, but there were just so many of them. I spit them into the wastebasket and took a quick swig of Diet Coke. "Oh, *really?*" I said, infusing the reply with as much sarcasm as possible. I chuckled, happy to play along with Catherine's prank.

"Yes," she said, "and please don't hang up." She hurried to explain that she was calling on behalf of President Bush, who wanted me to come and meet with him. As she spoke, offering details about the wishes of the president and the nature of the visit, I leaned forward in my desk chair. *She sure sounds like someone who's had to convince doubters before.*

My disbelief shifted to skepticism, and finally to outright amazement. *This is the real deal*, I thought. *I really am on the phone with the White House!* So much for a prank call. Within minutes, I found myself consenting to a trip to Washington. I pulled out my calendar, and we agreed on a date.

"One more thing," I said, just before we hung up. "I have to bring a wheelchair with me. I want President Bush to see this wheelchair we give away."

The woman paused. It would be difficult to arrange, she explained, and she warned that it was unlikely I'd be allowed to bring it inside. "If I come to the White House," I told her, "I'm going to bring a wheelchair."

We said our goodbyes, and the call was disconnected. *Don*, I thought, *it looks like you and your wheelchair are going to Washington.*

As it turned out, President Bush's staff learned about Free Wheelchair Mission through our participation in a documentary by the Challenged Athletes Foundation called *Emmanuel's Gift*. I bought an inexpensive blue suit, flew to Washington with my wheelchair, and, together with the foundation representatives, made my way to the White House.

It was just before one o'clock and sweltering hot.

We crossed the street and stopped at the X-ray machine at the guard gate. "You can't bring a wheelchair," the guard said, eyeing my awkward cargo. "It's not going to fit through the machine." I was frustrated but ready to relent. Obviously, my desire to bring my wheelchair to the meeting did not make it to the security guards. Had they known, they probably had other entries to the White House. I guess my determination made an impression on them. They sensed the urgency and resorted to an age-old alternative—a dog's sense of smell.

"Yes, I know, but there's got to be another way to do this," I said. "I have a meeting with the president at one o'clock, and I'm not leaving without this wheelchair."

The guard pulled out a phone and summoned a canine unit. Within minutes, two large men with German shepherds arrived. One of the men ordered the dog to sniff my chair.

"It's clean," the dog's handler said. "You can take it ahead."

We walked through the gate and into a side door that brought us right to the Oval Office. The entrance was a pair of French doors, one of which looked like it hadn't been opened in decades. I tried to muscle the wheelchair through the open half of the doorway, but it just wouldn't fit. The president's assistant stood on a chair, trying unsuccessfully to open the rusted latch.

"Sir," she said, "I don't think I can get this open."

"I'm bringing the chair with me," I insisted. "So we have to figure something out."

Not long after she called for backup, a six-foot-eight Marine appeared. He reached up and forced it open, flipping the rusted door latch like it was nothing. I then rolled my wheelchair into the outer vestibule of the Oval Office.

We waited a few minutes until the president's assistant announced that it was time for us to meet him. But my wheelchair wouldn't fit through the door to the Oval Office. After banging it on the door frame several times, I looked up and saw that the president was waiting for us, watching us. Not wanting to waste his time, I left the chair outside the door and walked in to meet President George W. Bush.

The office looked like a museum, just like in the movies. There wasn't a modern thing in sight, the most high-tech technology being an old grandfather clock, the kind you have to wind by hand. A Remington bronze sat on a small wooden table. My eyes followed it up to the giant portrait of George Washington.

The president seemed very relaxed. I was surprised how muscular he appeared to be. He had a terrible wound on one of his knuckles, I noticed, causing me to remember reading about a bicycle accident he'd been involved in at a meeting in Scotland.

President Bush began the meeting by speaking to the members from the Challenged Athletes Foundation. Then, he turned and looked directly at me.

"So," he asked, "what's going on with you?"

"Well," I said, "we started a nonprofit a couple of years ago called Free Wheelchair Mission, and we give away wheelchairs to people in developing countries, following God's Word." Then I explained how there are seventy-five million people in the world who need wheelchairs and often live on the ground, and that wheelchairs are typically too expensive for them to get.

"I don't think God wants them to live on the ground," I said, "and I don't think you do either."

The president looked interested. "Did you bring a wheelchair?" he asked.

"Yes, actually. I tried to bring in a wheelchair. It's out in the hall, but I can't get it through this door."

Don Schoendorfer

The president spoke with his aide, and within a minute, my wheelchair suddenly appeared in the Oval Office. Someone had rolled it through a door hidden in the wall.

President Bush examined the chair. "This is fantastic," he said. "Tell me about it."

"It's just a chair with wheels," I said. "I just want to get basic transportation for people. And we give these away for free, so we can't have them cost what wheelchairs made in the United States cost. It's just a wheelchair for people so they don't have to crawl on the ground."

The president looked at the frame and wheels, studying the simple design. "We want people to know that this is a gift from God," I continued. "We want to treat people like human beings who are created and loved by God."

We talked for a few more minutes, and I mentioned the wheelchairs that we had shipped to Iraq, aided by the US Army.

"Do you ever get any into Afghanistan?" he asked.

"We tried, a couple of years ago. We sent two containers there, but they got stuck in Pakistan. We received a wired message wanting a payment, then another requesting a larger payment, so we didn't know what to do."

"Do you want me to look into it for you?" the president asked.

I very much did.

He asked me to send his aide the paper trail of the shipping containers and the information about our contacts in Pakistan. Then the conversation ended. A photographer snapped a few pictures of us and off we went, rolling the wheelchair through the hidden door and out of the building.

Two weeks later, early in the morning, my phone rang. It was our partner in Afghanistan. He sounded upset.

"Don! These two containers of wheelchairs just pulled up beside my house without any notice, and I don't have anybody to help me unload them!"

I chuckled and shook my head. "Well, I'm sorry," I said. "They're compliments of President Bush."

About a month later, I was sitting back in my office in the first prototype of my wheelchair, which I used for an office chair. My cheeks again full of baby carrots, I noticed an official-looking letter in the stack of mail on my desk, addressed to Free Wheelchair Mission. The return address: The White House, Washington, DC. I tore open the envelope, and out slipped a check for $10,000 from President Bush.

I ran my hand along the arms of the white resin lawn chair, amazed by its journey, amazed how an antique wheelchair from the time of President Lincoln could inspire the development of a chair that would end up in the Oval Office of the White House.

———————

Not all the work we were doing with Free Wheelchair Mission was marked by high moments, though. We experienced lows as well, both in our organization and in our family, and soon, I would learn exactly how very low things could get.

26

CURSE

Irvine, California
September 2005

Following the trip to the White House, our organization continued to grow. The work was oftentimes grueling—physical-
ly, yes, but even more so emotionally. My engineering mind
kept me focused on the wheelchair logistics, but Laurie opened her
heart widely to every recipient we met.

Laurie was a cofounder of Free Wheelchair Mission and had been
involved in planning the strategy and tactics of the organization from
its inception. As our organization grew, her selfless love made her an
ideal partner, compelling her to jump in with her hands raised, willing
to do anything it took to show people how much God loves them.

She dove feet first into the work we were doing. She was the sort
of volunteer that most organizations dream of recruiting. Our three
girls participated in our mission trips as well, freely giving of their
own time and resources to help the people they met in countries far
from their home in Orange County.

Several months after I returned from Washington, Laurie was at work one afternoon at the Social Security Administration when she and several female colleagues decided they should all get mammograms. It would be a fun rite of passage, a bonding experience for the women who all enjoyed working together.

When Laurie's turn arrived, she sat motionless as the X-ray technician scanned her chest. Little did we know how life changing that scan would be. When the phone rang the next afternoon, Laurie fielded the call and then immediately called me. The radiologist had discovered a suspicious spot, and her doctor wanted her to undergo more testing. In that follow-up procedure, a separate spot was found in her lungs. Laurie had cancer, and it had begun to spread.

Even in the midst of an alarming medical challenge, Laurie's optimism broke through. As we sat at the kitchen table, processing the news of this diagnosis and talking through its implications for our family, Laurie marveled at the way God had directed our path.

If our daughter hadn't struggled with an eating disorder, we wouldn't have been brought to our knees, surrendering to God and asking for His assistance. We wouldn't have been brought back to church, with God challenging our thoughts about our purpose. If we'd had ample money in the bank, there would have been no reason for Laurie to go back to work when it was time for me to focus on Free Wheelchair Mission. And if Laurie had not returned to work, she wouldn't have been in the room when her colleagues all decided to have mammograms.

Somehow, God had used our daughter's eating disorder to reveal Laurie's cancer and give her another chance to live. And it seemed to me that if God could do that, could transform painful experiences into life-saving opportunities, then He could do anything.

Don Schoendorfer

God had been working in our lives all along, even when we didn't know it.

———————

Free Wheelchair Mission was changing lives around the world, and it was changing my own family, as well. There were so many others who had joined in the work we were doing, and despite Laurie's grim diagnosis, we knew it had to continue.

Dr. Susan Shore, a professor in Azusa Pacific University's Department of Physical Therapy, and her students helped us develop training materials to accompany our wheelchairs. They created a guide that covers everything from how to prevent pressure sores to recovery from falls and safe methods for transfer in and out of the wheelchair.

Dr. Shore also conducted a study assessing the quality of life of Free Wheelchair Mission recipients before and after receiving a chair. Her study results concluded that "recipient evaluation of the Free Wheelchair Mission wheelchair in two different countries has shown a positive, cost-effective benefit to both health and function without unusual risk."

We were elated.

As we gave away container after container of wheelchairs, I began thinking about ways to improve the chair. Our wheelchair was multipurpose, designed with mountain bike wheels for use in rugged terrain, and provided basic mobility to a broad range of recipients. However, it wasn't adjustable. This meant that there were people who, for reasons related to their small stature or specific physical challenges, needed extra postural support that our wheelchair couldn't provide.

In 2006, I called David Constantine, a man I'd met at a wheelchair conference. He was the founder of Motivation, a nonprofit in the United Kingdom that helps people with mobility disabilities, and he had been using a wheelchair since a tragic diving accident in Australia in 1982.

David agreed to help me come up with an inexpensive, adjustable chair. We worked together, communicating by email and phone, and with his engineering team came up with a design for a second-generation wheelchair.

We flew to China to visit the factory and had a prototype within a week. Laurie became a test subject, rolling the wheelchair over curbs at different angles to make sure it didn't tip. Our neighbor's four-year-old daughter became the model for an accessory that would allow a child to use the chairs.

The new wheelchair was designed with adjustability in mind, allowing for a more customized fit to address every recipient's individual needs. In our design, we'd included two independent footrests that could each be adjusted to accommodate any combination of different leg lengths.

We painted the wheelchair steel blue—a happy, soothing color. Also, we decided to include with every chair a wrench, air pump, patch kit, and recipient manual for home maintenance, along with contact information for local resources should service, maintenance, further training, or information be needed. We were even able to secure FDA clearance for our new "GEN_2" wheelchair, something we'd never had before.

Four years later, we partnered again with David Constantine, this time to design a wheelchair with the added benefit of being foldable. The "GEN_3," as it would be known, would address many of the needs we'd seen in the field. It was designed for better home storage and would be much easier to transport.

The training we offered addressed the technical aspects of using our wheelchairs, but it also went deeper. We required that our distribution partners go through a training that covered information about how to assemble and use the wheelchair, and we also required that they spend significant time learning about what causes disability. The need for this kind of training became painfully obvious to us during a grim, gut-wrenching experience in Uganda.

One of our distribution partners, a man named Francis Mugwanya, had traveled to a small village in his native Uganda where he met a family with a young boy who had lost his mobility due to polio. The child's relatives and neighbors believed the disability must have meant that he'd been cursed. They'd made efforts to appeal to the devil, to appease him with superstitious offerings. When that failed to break the spell, they decided to call a shaman to handle the situation.

With limited medical tools, the witch doctor instructed the parents to hold down the child. Francis listened to the boy's parents recount the violent episode, shocked by what he heard next: the shaman proceeded to gouge out the young child's eye. As the boy screamed and the family watched in horror, the man attempted to "cure" the disability—which he believed was a curse. Francis looked at the boy, saw the sunken hollow where his eye once was, prayed with the boy, and then gave him his very own wheelchair.

Whenever we encountered families in these types of situations, it was important to Francis and me that we do more than just provide a wheelchair. Additionally, we knew that something must be done to combat the erroneous idea that a disability is a sign of being cursed. Even in countries with large Christian populations, people with disabilities are often barred from entering churches because of the false assumption that because God cursed the ground (Genesis 3:17), anything or anyone who crawls on the ground, including people with disabilities, must also be cursed. In our training, we explained that disability is not a curse at all. We described the various medical reasons why some people have disabilities.

Perhaps most importantly, we wanted every recipient of our wheelchairs to know this:

Jesus Christ loves you. That's why you are receiving this wheelchair. We believe that this wheelchair comes from God. He created you, and He loves you as His child, just as you are. As believers in Jesus, we are called upon to serve others. Our prayer is that as you move around, you too will trust Him, serve Him, and bring glory to His name. God bless you.

27

REFLECTIONS

In the decade that followed, I became more and more aware of the incredible ways God was working in the life of our organization. One miracle became two, then three, and before I knew it, I had a long list of miracles God had accomplished as He established and grew Free Wheelchair Mission: the woman in Morocco; God sending Laurie into my life; our daughter developing an eating disorder that brought us to a treatment center where we heard a message from the Bible; Ethentica going bankrupt; the Fool's Game illustration at Mariners Church; the medical mission trip to India; the generous people in the Mariners congregation; finding a manufacturer in China; my first presentation yielding a strategic plan and enough funds to ship our first container of wheelchairs; the phone call with Pastor Robert in Peru; meeting President Bush; Indra being able to go to school; and countless others.

Once I surrendered to God and recognized Him as my real boss, I couldn't help but see each of these events as evidence that He'd been working behind the scenes all along.

Free Wheelchair Mission, which began as a simple blueprint in my garage in Santa Ana, had blossomed into a remarkable nonprofit organization that God was using to change the world—one person, one family, and one community at a time.

I'd begun with only the inception of a design, an engineering solution that I thought would make for an interesting academic paper. But God had different ideas.

Since my early days poring over my dog-eared copy of *Nonprofit Kit for Dummies*, so many people had joined us on this journey. Free Wheelchair Mission had grown into a professional and well-run organization, and we began to see that it was making a significant difference in the world.

From our humble beginnings with those first four wheelchairs that I took to India, distributing the best I knew how, we were now shipping five hundred wheelchairs per container to highly motivated and trained distribution partners. They were well equipped to receive, assemble, fit, and give the chairs to those in need, along with training those recipients to use and maintain their newfound means of mobility.

By 2010, we'd given away more than half a million wheelchairs, and the number just kept growing.

Over the years since the development of my rudimentary prototype in the garage, so many people have joined the cause and walked alongside me. Our donor base, which began with a single check for our first container of wheelchairs, now includes thousands of individuals, churches, and organizations. These donors—men, women, and children across the country—have made a powerful

Don Schoendorfer

difference, transforming countless lives by sharing their time, talents, and treasures.

We also now have an incredibly gifted staff who are dedicated to the mission, along with fifty-four partners on the ground in thirty-four countries around the world. Every one of these people has their own story to tell, stories of how the mission has impacted their own lives as they impact the lives of so many others.

One man who is making his own impact through Free Wheelchair Mission is George Hage, a retired occupational therapist in Boise, Idaho.

George and his wife, Renée, have worked with refugees in Boise for more than twenty years, and they began to feel a desire to help people with physical disabilities in the developing world. George connected with Free Wheelchair Mission and made it his own mission to raise funds to purchase more than thirty-six thousand wheelchairs—one for every seat in Albertsons Stadium at Boise State University. George knows that when we inspire others to give back, we can join together to make the world a better place. Some of these gifts will be monumental, like George Hage's, but others will be the simple act of providing one wheelchair to one person in need.

Another supporter who has carved out a significant place with Free Wheelchair Mission is Jim Franklin. Jim has been a copilot for Laurie and me since 2003, and his closet is full of the many different hats he has worn. He began as a supporter, then a volunteer, then a board member, and finally as the chairman of our board, a position he held for more than a decade. His involvement with Free Wheelchair Mission has even been a bit unconventional at times, such as when he assumes the role of auctioneer at our annual fundraiser. Jim knows our audience well and can both entertain and challenge our supporters. In fact, he challenges and stimulates all of us. In my own life, one not marked by an overwhelming abundance of friendships, I consider Jim one of my closest friends.

Each of us has the ability to serve where we are and with whatever resources we have.

I'm continually amazed at how far Free Wheelchair Mission has come. I think back to our first Miracle of Mobility fundraising event with the King of Ghana, an evening that set the stage for our more recent ones at the Segerstrom Center for the Arts—an enormous opera-house-style theater that seats thousands. We've been blessed to have keynote speeches by people like quarterback Tim Tebow, Paralympian swimmer Victoria Arlen, and Swati Mandela, the granddaughter of Nelson Mandela.

If you see a photo of me at any of these events, you'll see me in one of the many ethnic shirts I've collected on my travels over the years. I enjoy highlighting the beautiful cultural diversity of our world, and you know I've never been one to shy away from colorful clothing.

Over the years, we've partnered with professionals and engaged in ongoing innovation in order to keep our costs low and to continue to improve our wheelchair for recipients. From our first GEN_1 wheelchair design, we developed the GEN_2 and GEN_3 chairs and, eventually, a remarkable wheelchair test track in April 2017.

I smile when I think back to Skip Lanfried's test of my first prototype in the parking lot of Mariners Church. With our test track, we're now able to test four wheelchairs at a time, simulating the rugged conditions in developing countries. This allows us to push our chairs to their breaking points to see where we can make improvements in comfort and longevity.

I gave considerable thought to what we should call the test track. After several days, the only name that seemed fitting was "Lotus," named for Lotus Blossom, the little girl in India who received one of my very first wheelchairs so many years ago. I've thought of her often over the years and, through our contacts at Christian Missions Charitable Trust who first hosted us when we were in India, I received periodic updates on how she and her family were doing.

"She wants to come to Sunday School," they'd tell me. "She wants to learn more about Christianity . . . and she's trying to learn how to walk."

Walk? I'd think. *What do you mean, she's trying to learn to walk?*

Those conversations went on for several years, and every six months or so I'd get an update. Evidently, Lotus Blossom was using her GEN_1 wheelchair as a walker to raise herself up and train herself to stand.

In 2015, fourteen years after I first met Lotus Blossom, the nonprofit educational organization Visionaries Inc. approached me about featuring Free Wheelchair Mission in a television series that would premiere on PBS. When I told them about Lotus, they instantly wanted her to be part of their show, and I shared with them footage from a trip we had taken back to India the year before.

The morning after our flight arrived in Chennai, we had driven to the slum where Lotus and her family lived. The river was still there, but the garbage dump was gone. As we approached the area, I heard someone call my name. Looking around, I lifted my eyes to the second story of the tenement and saw Lotus motioning for us to come upstairs.

It was there that she and her mother shared with us a remarkable story.

For years, Lotus was determined to learn how to walk. She would pull herself up on the back of the wheelchair, try to take a step, and then fall over. Again and again she did this, hurting herself because her atrophied legs just didn't have the muscular strength to support her body.

Unable to bear the sight of her daughter's repeated injuries, Lotus's mother would take away the wheelchair. But Lotus would always find it again. Each day, when her mother left home to rummage through the trash heap, Lotus would pull out the wheelchair and try again. Her desire to walk was all-consuming.

On their visits to Lotus's home every three or four months, members of Christian Missions Charitable Trust would hear the mother express her frustrations.

"You have to get this chair out of here," she said on one of their visits. "She's possessed. The chair is a demon. It's her brain. She thinks she's going to walk, but she's hurting herself."

"We know what you can do," the mission worker said. "You should pray."

"To whom?" she asked. In India, there are reportedly some 330 million gods to choose from.

"Pray to the God of all gods, the One who brought the wheelchair in the first place."

And so, Lotus's mother began to pray, asking God to help her daughter to stop hurting herself, asking God to heal her legs so she could walk. The neighbors in the river slum saw Lotus's mother's despair. They saw her emotion as she cried out to God. And then another miracle happened.

They started praying as well.

For more than a year, the community prayed, until one day, to everyone's astonishment, Lotus took her first step.

"I don't know how to explain this!" her mother said to Christian Missions Charitable Trust on their next visit.

"We do," they said. "It's a miracle. The God who brought this chair to India wanted Lotus Blossom to learn how to walk. But He also wanted you to believe in Him."

Because of Lotus's miracle, which began with a simple wheelchair, Lotus and her mother were both baptized, along with dozens of others who lived in their neighborhood. A Christian community was born in this slum, a community rich in faith that continues to this very day.

28

FLOR

Ayacucho, Peru
April 2017

From the back seat of the white pickup truck, I watched the green hills of Peru. Directly behind us was a silver sedan, its wheels making dusty the road that curved around the jagged terrain.

We were traveling deep into the Andes mountains toward the city of Ayacucho, two hundred miles from the coast of the South Pacific Ocean. The city had gained the nickname "city of churches" for its thirty-three Christian churches, each representing one year of Jesus's life.

But the indigenous Quechuans had a nickname for this city, too: "Death"—a name that became more understandable to me as we drove through the muddy streets and dilapidated slums.

Since the 1970s, the people of Ayacucho had suffered greatly at the hands of the Shining Path, a Communist organization known for terrorizing the population with guerrilla tactics in their violent attempt to incite a revolution. Several years had passed since that organization had been disassembled, but in the minds of the Peruvians, the memories were still very much alive; the scars were still visible all over the city.

I had flown into Ayacucho on the previous day to rendezvous with a team of volunteers who had been helping us assemble and distribute wheelchairs in Peru since 2003. They belong to a church called Camino de Vida, or "the Way of Life." Next to me in the truck sat Pastor Robert Barriger, a man who has dedicated his life to serving the people of Peru through random acts of kindness, or what he calls a "serve-olution."

Leaving for Peru felt like the lowest possible point of my life. Laurie was so weak—all of her energy had been used up in fighting her cancer—and she'd spent much of the past few months in the hospital. Our daughters and I visited her multiple times a day, and I had even set up a mobile office in the corner of her hospital room. This trip had been planned for months, but now, even though Laurie was back at home, I didn't want to go. I didn't want to leave her—she was just too sick. Everyone said I needed to be in Peru, but I resisted mightily.

Laurie had been a board member since the beginning, though, and she knew all about the planned trip. She knew how significant this one was. In addition to being my wife and best friend, Laurie was my partner in life and in Free Wheelchair Mission. She would have given anything to go with me, but she was also a realist. Few people knew her cancer was killing her, and she hid her pain well.

"If you can't bring yourself to do this for *you*," she said, "then you need to do this for me." So I arranged for two of her dear friends, Cindy and Ellen, to travel from the East Coast to keep her company.

I tried to contain my emotions as I said goodbye. I felt tears welling in my eyes as a warm smile spread across Laurie's face. It was a smile I'd seen thousands of times over the last forty years, and my heart caught in my throat as I turned and walked out the door.

Ayacucho was an ancient land, a place that held importance for countless civilizations, harkening back thousands of years before the Incan Empire to the earliest known human settlements on the continent. It was a place marked with poverty, and the longer we drove, the more poverty we saw.

I could feel the pavement turn to dirt as our two-vehicle caravan left the outskirts of Ayacucho, slowing occasionally for the large tractor, dog, or farm animal in our path. The sky was overcast when we departed, but by noon, when we arrived, white clouds had formed along the base of the mountains, cushioning their slopes, separating sky from earth and revealing our destination: a remote village.

Laurie had come with me on so many vision trips before. My attention was always on the wheelchairs, but hers was always on the recipients. No matter how old, how young, how clean, how dirty, or how much their disabilities made them asocial, she would throw her arms around them, hug them, hold their hands, and look into their eyes with her trademark loving smile. I dare say she melted tens of thousands of hearts over the years. She told them how God loved them, and she did it in such a way that they truly believed it.

Laurie would have loved to witness this day. This was a huge milestone for our mission, a day that we'd dreamt about for a long time, the bittersweet culmination of decades of hard work. But as the truck came to a halt, I knew that this was more than just a special occasion for Free Wheelchair Mission. It was more than just a milestone.

We had come to give away our one-millionth wheelchair.

This chair was a memorial to the one million lives that God had forever changed with a gift of mobility. The seed planted so long ago in Morocco had not only blossomed into a blueprint for a wheelchair that had changed the lives of so many, but it now brought me face to face with a twelve-year-old girl named Flor, meaning "Flower."

"She woke up this morning," Pastor Robert said to me, just before we exited the truck, "and her life was one thing. It will never be the same."

Sixteen of the villagers were waiting for us, sitting in a line of chairs in front of a pink-walled building. With the help of a few volunteers, we unloaded the assembled wheelchair from the back of the truck and brought it over to Flor, who was sitting beside her mother.

When Flor saw us coming, her eyes suddenly lit up, and a smile broke out on her face, followed by a loud laugh that I could hear all the way from the truck. Flor's story, not unlike the stories of so many others I'd heard, was marked by tragedy.

When she was an infant, her temperature spiked, resulting in a severe case of meningitis that went untreated because her parents didn't have enough money to take her to the hospital. Her condition affected her neurological function and ultimately impaired her ability to walk.

As we wheeled the chair closer, the villagers all stood to their feet to greet us, some clapping. Flor couldn't stand up with them, however. I could see the redness welling up in her eyes, beneath her dark-brown bangs.

For people who live on the ground—for those who spend their days crawling on their stomachs, whether their immobility is the result of chronic malnutrition, disease, systemic poverty, or war—the first thing they see when you walk up to them is your shoes. It makes them feel helpless, like you could just step on their fingers without even noticing. Then comes the dust kicked up by your shoes. It drifts into their faces and gets in their eyes, exposing them to germs and bacteria that live on the ground.

When you give a wheelchair to someone in the developing world, you never know how many years, or decades, you instantly add to their lives. The simple act of getting them up off the ground and out of the dirt increases the duration and quality of their lives. Not only does it give them a fighting chance of survival, but it also restores to them their dignity, their humanity. And for the first time in their lives, what once seemed impossible, like education and self-sustenance, suddenly becomes a reality for many of them.

Flor was strong enough to hold herself up, we learned. If someone placed her by a wall or doorframe, she could support the weight of her body with her arms. But thus far in her life, her only mode of mobility was her mother, a petite woman who carried her daughter piggyback-style on her shoulders.

I watched Flor wrap her arms around her mother's neck, her feet dangling only a few inches above the ground. It was a temporary form of mobility, especially because her mother would only grow older, and Flor would only grow taller and heavier.

When we approached, I helped Flor's mother lift her up and put her in the blue wheelchair. "He will show you how to use it," one of the volunteers said.

"Do you like it?" asked her mother.

Flor looked up at all of us, all smiles now. "I like it!" she said, squealing with laughter as her father began pushing the wheelchair across the grass. "Bueno! Bueno!" she exclaimed, clapping with enthusiasm in the sheer bliss of the moment. Then she reached down and began rolling the wheels by herself, with her own arms, without anyone's help, moving over the ground on her own for the very first time in her life.

The emotion of that experience spread over all of us. Everyone in the village was either crying or clapping, including Flor's father, who walked over to us and said, with the help of a translator, "I'm so grateful for all of you, from my heart, for supporting me and my little girl."

It was a moment sixteen years in the making, one that I can still feel to this very day.

After we said our goodbyes, we returned to our vehicles to embark on the journey back to Ayacucho. But as we were leaving the cluster of buildings in the village, something unexpected caught my eye.

It was a house. I didn't remember seeing it on the way there, but I couldn't take my eyes off it. There was nothing unusual about its clay-brick construction or its roof, which was made of curved tiles. But unlike all the other buildings we had seen that day, this house had one noticeable exception: a bright, blue-painted front door.

The door looked out of place among the brown walls and pale earth around it, like a patch of sky stamped through the ground.

As we traveled over the bumpy roads and along the mountain ridges to the city, I thought about that door, about that color, about the whole experience of the day. Over the years, I've seen a lot of suffering in villages just like that one, a lot of poverty and disease.

And yet, there was that bright blue door, standing tall on its hinges as a symbol of *life* in the midst of Death. It was the same cheerful blue as the GEN_3 wheelchair, a color that represents hope, opportunity, and freedom.

There was a time in my life when I wanted to be a billionaire. But the real treasure, I came to discover, was far more valuable. It was people.

And that's the legacy I'd like to leave the world: to open doors of possibility for those who cannot walk, to lift them up, give them mobility, and tell them, "When you're in this wheelchair, we want you to feel like you're in God's hands, that He's protecting you."

That night, as I returned to Ayacucho and prepared to fly back to California, I went to sleep, turning over the events of the day. Free Wheelchair Mission had given away its one-millionth wheelchair. But even though this chapter had come to a close, I prayed the story would continue. There was still so much work to be done. There are still millions of people just like Flor, and Lotus Blossom, and Indra, and Emmanuel, and many others who desperately need the gift of mobility.

AFTERWORD

Just over a month after our trip to Peru, where we gave away our millionth wheelchair, Laurie succumbed to her cancer following a valiant battle of more than a decade. Her life was filled with countless sacrifices and immeasurable love that extended to the neediest of this world. She never missed an opportunity to make sure that every wheelchair recipient knew that they were in God's hands. Even near the end, as Laurie's strength faded and we knew that her time on earth was short, we felt at peace because we, too, were safe in God's hands.

I thought back to our experience together in Morocco, standing on the street corner, watching the poor woman drag her small, beleaguered body across the dirt. Laurie had been with me since the beginning, and without her, Free Wheelchair Mission never would have existed. God knew how much our girls and I, along with the countless people without mobility all around the world, needed her. Through Laurie's life, God changed the world and me.

God also worked through my daughter's life. She struggled with her eating disorder for years, trying different programs that didn't seem to work. Ultimately, it was the brilliance of one of her medical professionals who created a custom program that helped her achieve victory. I use the word "victory" because someone with an eating disorder cannot eliminate food from their life in the same way that someone can eliminate alcohol, drugs, etc. The journey that led to my daughter's victory also led to God's victory over my heart, which started with the visit to the treatment facility in Arizona and continues to this day.

In the same way my daughter's doctor took a unique approach to her situation, my education allowed me to look at problems differently than a lot of people do when they develop a new concept. That was what motivated me to start this whole endeavor. We needed a more efficient, effective solution to a gargantuan problem.

At Free Wheelchair Mission, we think holistically about our mission. It begins with the engineering of the wheelchair and extends to the emotional well-being of the recipient, to the joy it brings to the recipient's family and community, and, ultimately, to making the world a better place.

I often ask people, "What could someone give you that would significantly change your life?" Some attempt to answer this question, but most don't even try. If you had asked me that question earlier in my life, I would have told you that I wanted to earn a billion dollars, but today, I don't think the money would change my life that much. I already have the things that I need. I'm already content.

But for someone who lives each day secluded in a dark room, a thoughtfully designed and properly fitted wheelchair—coupled with effective training—can change their entire life. Mobility is not a luxury, it's a necessity, and everyone who needs a wheelchair should have the opportunity to get one.

The older I get, the more aware I become that my own chapter, my own journey in this world, will also come to an end. In recent years, a frequent question posed to me has been, "When are you going to write your book?" In defense, I would reply, "The story isn't over yet." And this is true, but it wasn't my only reason. The real reason is that I am not comfortable when the focus is on me. This book is about us surrendering to God, trusting Him, and taking direction from Him. We can all be involved in His mission. My prayer is that by sharing a few stories of my life in these pages, you will discover your own blueprints for life, your own contributions to humanity, and your own calling and purpose within the kingdom of God, no matter how big or small.

Since the day Flor was lifted into her miracle wheels in 2017, we have continued our work, even in the face of a global pandemic and other international challenges. Over the past two decades, Free Wheelchair Mission has distributed wheelchairs to over 1.3 million people living in ninety-four countries across five continents. But our work is far from over.

Right now, there are still seventy-five million people around the world who are forced to live on the ground, and less than 10 percent of those people will ever have access to a wheelchair. As we move into the future, our next goal is to ensure that our second million wheelchair recipients feel the same relief, comfort, joy, and freedom that comes from a God who loves them.

Something unique happens when you give a person a wheelchair—it's a moment of indescribable transformation. When you lift them off the ground and place them in the chair for the first time, a bright new future suddenly opens up for them. It's such a powerful experience. When they go outside, often for the first time, and see people looking them eye to eye, they start thinking, "Maybe I *can* get to school. Maybe I *can* get a job. Maybe I *can* go to church. Maybe I *can* visit friends who used to visit me but who aren't coming over anymore. Maybe my husband, my parents, my neighbors *can* go get their jobs since they won't have to focus their life on taking care of my needs." I have seen firsthand that the gift of mobility not only transforms the lives of the individuals who receive the wheelchairs, but also the lives of countless other family members, caregivers, and community members. One wheelchair truly becomes miracle wheels.

Right now, more than ever, those living with disabilities in developing countries urgently need our support. In times of worldwide pandemic, disaster, emergency, or crisis, people living with disabilities in the developing countries we serve are often hit the hardest. The work we do in giving away wheelchairs enables us not only to save lives by offering mobility, but also to become conduits for other forms of kindness, such as helping people secure access to food, water, and medical care. For years now, we've been providing mobility aids and other critical medical and surgical supplies to our distribution partners and caregivers serving in these communities. Then, when the need arose, we also began supplying masks, gloves, and PPE.

The loss of mobility changes everything. But the gift of mobility *also* changes everything.

That's why I tell our story, not only to share my life with you, but also to encourage you to share your life with someone else. I'd like to invite you to join us in this vision, in this mission. Join the thousands of volunteers, staff, and donors as we together continue to seek to restore hope, dignity, and mobility to those who need it most.

You don't have to help a million people to change the whole world. Start by changing *one* person's whole world. And then that one becomes two . . . and then three. Together, we can lift so many and give them the transformative gift of mobility.

As of this writing, for only about a dollar a day, you can help transform the lives of four people per year with the gift of four wheelchairs. Four sets of miracle wheels. Each year, you can help transform the lives of those in need, just like Lotus Blossom, Julia, and Flor. And with each life you help to transform around the world, you just might discover, as I have over so many years, that it'll transform *your* whole world, too.

HOW TO GET INVOLVED

FREEWHEELCHAIRMISSION.ORG

In addition to the blessing of seeing many lives being transformed by the gift of mobility, I have also been blessed to see many lives being transformed here in the US and around the world by *giving* the gift of mobility.

At Free Wheelchair Mission, we are thankful for the support of tens of thousands who have been called to help us through the years by providing their time, talent, and treasure. They have been touched by the stories of transformation and want to be a part of creating and sharing some miracle wheel stories of their own.

I'm often asked, "How can I help?" or "What is the best way for me to help?"

One of the easiest and most important ways to help is to visit our website at FreeWheelchairMission.org and donate wheelchairs to those in need. Whether it's one wheelchair, or two, or twenty, or a hundred, any amount and any number will transform lives.

Even better than giving one time is to come with us in our journey over the long term by joining our monthly giving program. While not everyone can provide twenty wheelchairs at once, perhaps you could commit to giving four wheelchairs a year for five years. Giving monthly helps us in so many ways, including making our operations and forecasting more efficient.

Along with giving financially, there are many ways to help.

Here are twelve ways you can get involved today:

1. Join our Mobilize monthly giving program. For just about a dollar per day, you can transform the lives of four people per year, or twenty people over five years.

2. Sign up for our email newsletters. Each week, you will hear about our work and receive stories about the many lives being transformed with the gift of mobility.

3. Follow us on social media. Look for the social media icons on our website and click to follow or like our pages on Facebook, Instagram, LinkedIn, YouTube, TikTok, and more.

4. Share this book with others. Pass the book along to family or friends. Or better yet, buy them copies of their own. Bring it to a small group or book club.

5. Volunteer with us. We often look for help with local events and crucial administrative tasks at our offices.

6. Become an Ambassador. We have hundreds of volunteers who help us to raise funds through their own creative fund-raising pages or team fundraising events.

7. Join #TeamMobility and the Move for Mobility. Participate in a virtual or in-person marathon, run, walk, bike, roll, kayak, or do any activity of choice in this customizable event.

8. Send wheelchairs as Christmas, holiday, or anytime gifts. On our website, we offer beautiful greeting cards that you can purchase and send to others. Your card recipients also get a gift card that allows them to "send" a wheelchair to someone in need around the world.

9. Invite your company, association, church, sports team, or other group to get involved. We have many ways that companies and groups can partner with us to help engage employees or group members and give the gift of mobility.

10. Watch or attend a Miracle of Mobility event. Each year, we have ways to watch our annual celebration and fundraising event, whether virtually or in person.

11. Give through stock transfers, workplace giving, or legacy gifts. Look for more information on our website for ways to give beyond one-time cash donations.

12. Pray. We appreciate your prayers for our mission, staff, and partners, but most importantly for those living with disabilities around the world who need our help. Our ongoing prayer is that everyone who needs a wheelchair will have one.

Please visit FreeWheelchairMission.org to learn more and to get involved.

Whether you can commit to all the items on this list or just one, we thank you! We would not be able to continue in this important mission without the generous support of so many like you.

DISCUSSION QUESTIONS

1. The opening of the book describes Don's first encounter with a woman who had lost her mobility and was crawling on the ground. Have you ever encountered a situation that had a profound impact on you and you experienced the urge to do something about it? What situation did you encounter, and how did it affect you?

2. We all have our own, unique stories. As you read Don's story, what parts resonated with your own? Does your own story point toward a particular purpose? How so?

3. In chapter 13, Don describes his struggle to find a place where he can contribute his time and talents to serve others, but he keeps drawing a blank. Have you had similar experiences? Or have you found a place where passion, purpose, and need intersect? Take a few minutes to talk through possible places of service in your own life.

4. Don mentions the World Health Organization's estimate of the need for wheelchairs as seventy-five million worldwide. Does this figure astound you? Do you believe we can make a difference when the need is so great? How?

5. On page 109, Don accepts that "this can't be a coincidence... This has to be providence." And on page 146, he says, "There was a time in my life when I'd use the word 'coincidence' to describe it. But listening to Father Winner describe what became of Indra and how she used her education made me prefer the word 'miracle' instead." What are your own thoughts on "coincidence," "providence," and "miracle"? What circumstances in your life could you describe as providence or miracle? Or are they all just coincidences?

6. In chapter 13, page 95, Don describes the "Fool's Game." What do you think about the pastor's message? What meaning does it have for you?

7. In Angola, Don is given an insight into serving people with disabilities in the developing world (page 160): "You are never going to have enough to meet the need." How do you feel about this challenge?

8. Don's story takes us from modest beginnings to a successful career, living the good life in Southern California. It takes some serious incidents to redirect his life's trajectory and bring him in contact with those who have so little. We are very blessed in the developed world, and it can be easy to take this for granted. In what ways do you use your own blessings to bless others? What would it take for more people to be aware of the needs outside of their bubble, and to use their blessings to help people who have far less?

9. Don made a surprising claim on page 212: "If you had asked me that question earlier in my life, I would have told you that I wanted to earn a billion dollars, but today, I don't think the money would change my life that much. I already have the things that I need." Have you ever wondered what you would do if you won or were given a billion dollars? How would you use it? How might it change your life? Should we even dream about having a billion dollars when, for less than a hundred dollars, a wheelchair can change somebody's life?

10. Having read Don's book, do you think you have a better understanding of the lives of people who lack mobility and may never be able to receive a wheelchair on their own? What can you do to make a difference for them?

ACKNOWLEDGMENTS

This book project was initiated because Free Wheelchair Mission was approaching the celebration of twenty years of transforming the lives of people with mobility disabilities, who are often marginalized in the developing world. As I reflect on the journey, I think of the many people who have walked alongside me in various ways and contributed so much toward improving the lives of others (and themselves). It's impossible to list them all, so please forgive me if I have failed to acknowledge your contribution below.

The place to start is, of course, in thanking the Lord for giving me gifts, and then showing me how to use them to build His kingdom. This is not *my* mission or *our* mission. This is *God's* mission, and we are blessed to be His hands. I like to say that God is my boss, and I like to live this way, too.

To my parents I owe the gifts of humility, from my father, and creativity, from my mother. Their modeling of hard work, perseverance, and ingenuity set me on the path to achieving a great education.

I'm also tremendously grateful for my family, who have been with me along the way. Laurie was the kind of lady most people only get the privilege of reading about, and I had her in my life for forty-five years. We were blessed with three wonderful daughters: Anna, Heidi, and Erika. They may never realize how much they helped the two of us to be better human beings—and the world to be a better place.

I owe my education to three amazing intellects: Asher Shapiro, Jerome Lettvin, and Steve Raymond.

When I think back to the transition from wheelchair concept to our first distribution success, I think of Karen Taulien, Skip Lanfried, and Mike Bayer. Thank you all for being there to help me with those early, significant steps.

These past twenty years, I've had the profound privilege of knowing spiritual leaders all around this world. They've helped me understand how God works, what He expects of me, and how to hear His voice. They include Kenton and Laurie Beshore, Jose in Angola, Father Winner, Robert Barringer, Bob Shank, Eric Heard, and George Hage.

Since the beginning, God has blessed me with a fantastic board of directors, men and women with experience and wisdom beyond my reach. I have gratitude for all of our board members, present and past, who freely gave their time to the expansion of the ministry, and I must mention several here: Stuart Rattray, Jim Franklin, Denny Kromer, Connie Salios, and Deborah Anderson.

There were, and still are, times when I have questioned myself and my capabilities. And there were many times when a brief discussion with Professor Susan Shore or George Duff made all the difference. To both of them, I am grateful.

None of this work could happen without support from our donors, and I am grateful to so many people for sharing their time, their talents, and their treasure.

Along the way, we have made significant improvements in the chairs we distribute, from GEN_1 to the current GEN_2 and GEN_3 wheelchairs. For these improvements, I thank David

Constantine of Motivation, and Ann Shen and Jose Yu of JAM, our wheelchair manufacturer.

One of the absolute key functions of Free Wheelchair Mission is the safe provision of wheelchairs, by way of our distribution partners, to recipients in ninety-four developing countries around the world. Were it not for these partners, Free Wheelchair Mission could never succeed. They are our presence, our hands and feet, in our destination countries.

As we round out these first twenty years, I am so grateful for our incredible Free Wheelchair Mission staff. Each member gives their very best to this mission. Each one of them puts their heart and soul into bringing mobility, dignity, and joy into the lives of our recipients.

Nuka Solomon, in particular, is more than our very powerful CEO—she is my partner.

Finally, this project and book would not have been completed without the help of Rebecca and Christian George in putting the story down on paper.

To these many people, and to countless others who have contributed over the years and will continue to contribute for years to come, I'll always be grateful.

ABOUT THE AUTHOR

D r. Don Schoendorfer is a biomedical engineer, inventor, entrepreneur, and humanitarian who lives in Santa Ana, California. Armed with an undergraduate degree from Columbia University and a PhD in mechanical engineering from MIT, Don spent nearly twenty-five years in the medical device industry, designing cutting-edge innovations resulting in more than sixty patents to his name.

After a life-changing encounter overseas, and with a strong sense of God's calling, Don founded Free Wheelchair Mission and has made it his mission to address the problem of mobility around the world, where 75 million people need wheelchairs but are unable to get one on their own. The innovative, cost-efficient line of wheelchairs that he developed and gave away for free—the "Miracle Wheels"—has transformed the lives of millions of people with disabilities.

Don's humanitarian work has garnered numerous awards and accolades, including ones from The White House, the United States House of Representatives, and The White House Congressional Medal of Honor Society.

When he is not busy tinkering with his inventions, Don enjoys spending time with his three daughters, two amazing granddaughters, and a Siberian Husky named Tolbi.